Undergraduate History Study - *The Guide to Success*

Gilbert Pleuger

ISBN 0 9515764 3 7

First published 1997

Impression number	10	9	8	7	6	5	4	3	2	1
Year			2001	2000	1999	1998	1997			

Cover by Stephen Odom and Gilbert Pleuger
Line portraits by Stephen Odom
Designed and set by Sempringham publishing services, Bedford
Sempringham publishing, PO Box 248, Bedford MK41 0ZU
Printed by Redwood Books, Trowbridge, Wiltshire

ii

Contents

My thanks are due to Michael Barlen and Charles Hay, both sadly deceased, and William Makin who indulged my interest in the arts of helping students succeed and furthered my involvement in the theory of History.

I record my thanks, also, to David Huxley, Robert Pearce and Michael Stanford, as well as Jane Huxley and Calum Pallister, both recently undergraduates, for their comments on the script. P. McFarland and John Plummer willingly offered valuable service in the preparation of the text.

Gilbert Pleuger

Acknowledgements

Blackwell Publishers for an extract from *On History and Other Essays* by Michael Oakeshott and extracts from *A Companion to the Study of History* by Michael Stanford; Jonathan Cape for extracts from *The Football Factory* by Jonathan King and *Flaubert's Parrot* by Julian Barnes.

List of figures

Welcome

WELCOME to your companion guide to undergraduate History and congratulations on gaining your place for degree course study. This guide is written to help you to be an effective student, to gain a high reward for your effort and to enjoy your study and undergraduate years. These intentions are met by the three main themes which run through the book: a *positive mindset* (so that you actively respond toward your opportunities in undergraduate life and study); attention to *strategy* (so that you take a longer view of your study tasks); and *study skills* - any one of which may not be decisive but, taken together, will greatly reshape your study procedure. You may think some of my suggestions are so minor they hardly matter. My answer is that lots of minor improvements, when taken together, will make a major advance. Even the world's largest ocean, the Pacific, is made up of only individual drops of water.

A Book of Suggestions, Not Prescriptions

It is easy to remain in a rut with work procedures. However well your methods work, better students are circumspect and open to improvements. This guide does not seek to prescribe how you should study but to offer suggestions which you can try in order to increase your study efffectiveness. The short chapters can be read in any order. Several chapters relate to others and I usually indicate this. In some chapters I begin with simpler procedures and go on to more sophisticated points, so if you decide that you have already mastered the suggestions don't dismiss the chapter straight away. While you may choose to read the book from beginning to end you will probably want to refer and re-refer to particular chapters over your years of study. There is no 'quick fix' for improved study effectiveness but changes in technique, practised and developed over weeks and months, together with a sound study strategy and positive mindset, will radically enhance your undergraduate years, enable you to achieve higher grades and to have a great time.

The Undergraduate Years

Y OU PROBABLY had to work hard to win your undergraduate place. So now you have at least three years of study for your degree. These years are an opportunity. What will you make of it?

Degree-course study enables you to study History, of whatever period or aspect, with greater depth and in a more interesting way. Your undergraduate years, also, give you more control over your time, more free time and great social and sport/leisure opportunities. Students who gain most from all these aspects of undergraduate life are normally those who, while keeping a balance between them, are busy in all three. By being busy with work, social life and sport/leisure you will go a good way to deal with a possible problem, the relative absence of externally imposed routine. Routine imposed by a busy life style need not remove flexibility and spontaneity in student life, a wonderful possibilty of the undergraduate years, but a busy life style fosters the development of the whole person. And that is the fundamental justification for your undergraduate years. When you receive your degree, you will have become a more complete and capable person who happens, also, to have studied History, gained a qualification and mastered the skills of history study - skills which you take with you for the rest of your life and which lead to success and satisfaction when applied in many careers. (History graduate opportunities are mentioned in Chapter 18.)

A Busy Life Style

For some of you, a busy life style will come naturally, but for others it will not. After all, students come together at college or university from so many directions there is no dominant student type. For students who do not readily take part in non-work activity, it is important to note that participation in sporting or social pursuits do not come to you. You have to go out to them. Going out to participate in activities is particularly useful in the first year because by the end of your first year, when you are one-third through your

A Busy Life Style

course, you will have established some sort of activity- and social-life pattern. Going out to join activities is made easier for many first year students who have college-provided accommodation on campus or near the university centre and its students' union and facilities. The pointer to fulfilling lives in post-graduation life and as a student is to have several segments of life 'on the move' at the same time, in the way a juggler keeps skittles in play.

Ground Work

Not all fresher students are fortunate enough to have comfortable college-provided accommodation - arrangements which will make sure you are with other students. For those students who are in digs alone, possibly a fair distance from college and its facilities, the need to be active and to go out for social life and leisure/sport with fellow students is far greater and may take a lot more effort. One reason for student ineffectiveness is isolation, whether in social life or study. The usefulness of discussion in connection with your work is mentioned in Chapter 4.

The other groundwork to consider is the physical conditions in which you live and work. If your digs are cold, or you have no desk light, or your chair is broken, or the neighbours are impossibly noisy until 3 am most nights (parties are fine twice a week but not every night), then you have to be *active* to change these conditions. Find the appropriate person and discuss the problem. As a last resort, you may have to move, but don't 'suffer in silence' because if your physical conditions of life and work are unsatisfactory you will not be able to be an effective student.

Apart from accommodation officers and maintenance departments, colleges usually allocate students to academic tutors and, sometimes, also to pastoral tutors. Usually, these days, colleges have a counselling service. So there are several people you can raise difficulties and problems with. There is nothing wrong with having a problem. The only thing that can be wrong is if you do not actively deal with it - with the help of others. A problem or a difficulty is itself an opportunity. Young people do not always recognise this. A broken shin bone is a problem - it stops you walking. But once it is put right, you can be as robust as if you had never had a problem. So there is nothing wrong with a problem or difficulty, it is an opportunity to take control and to rectify it.

Vacations

Your undergraduate terms are short: nearly half the year is vacation time. Here are some of the possible uses of vacations.

- Relaxation and recovery after term time.
- Time with family and friends.
- Study for missed topics or uncompleted assignments from the previous term.
- Checking out the local night life and a busy social life.
- Temporary employment to earn money.
- Work experience, possibly as unpaid assistant, in the occupation area in which you wish to work when you graduate.
- Travel, for pleasure, say to Bali or Thailand, or to develop your interests. This might mean a visit to Shining Path territory in Peru (inform the British Embassy of your intentions and keep in touch with your relations) or to the former Soviet Union.
- Participation in your leisure or sporting interests, whether potholing, squash or music.

If I was asked which was most important, I would reply like a politician and evade the question by saying that all are worthwhile and have importance. What especially matters is the balance between them. Too much time spent on one and the neglect of others will mean you miss opportunities. Students who become disappointed by the undergraduate years are those who either completely neglect one of the eight possibilities during their student vacations or who spend nearly all their time on only one. College vacations, like your degree course, are opportunities for you to expand your experiences and to grow as a person. As is indicated in Chapter 18, employment experience is particularly helpful to you when you make your first post-graduation job applications.

It is time now, in the following 12 chapters, to explore History study skills.

History Study

1 Reading and Noting

READING AND NOTING are central to advanced History study. Lectures, seminars, films, videos, CD-Roms or discussions are complementary to reading and noting and can help understanding but reading and noting are the core activities for the History student.

Review of Your Reading Style

The trouble with reading and noting, however, apart from the quantity that is necessary, is that you have done this for over 10 years and have an established procedure. Do you need to change your approach and methods for undergraduate study? We do not expect netball or football players to play the way they did in the primary school playground, or senior school team, when they reach the premier league: we take it for granted that they will develop their skills. The same is true for reading and noting. Because reading and noting are so central to History students' work, a review of your current methods is important. What are books for?

Selecting What to Read

The books you use contain information and ideas: they present an account of the past and ideas and analysis which associate events with other events. Sometimes a history book will present an argument. The good student will see books in this way, that is, as sources from which, if an *active* approach is taken, information and ideas can be gained efficiently. If you have this in mind, before you use a book, you will analyse and judge it. (There is further discussion of types of books in the next chapter.) How much of the book do you need to read to gain the central ideas? Sometimes the main idea is in the title of the book, as in *Society in Crisis. France in the Sixteenth Century* by J.H.M. Salmon (1975). The argument may be summarised in an introduction or conclusion - and steps in the argument summarised at the end or beginning of each chapter. A book's main themes may be mentioned in the publisher's comment on the back cover. The second place to look for the themes and analysis, and the structure of the book, is the contents page. Further, within a chapter, if there are subheadings they show the arrangement of the contents and may indicate the development of an argument. Most students may be used to selecting some chapters to read from a heavyweight textbook but the same selection should be applied to shorter, more specialised books. Even if you decide you need to follow the chapter in detail, do you need to read the whole chapter for you to extract the theme and key evidence? Last, don't forget that for particular information the index is invaluable. You have made a big step towards increased study effectiveness if you think about books as carriers of information and ideas: aim to 'duck and weave' in order to take what you want, and not treat it as a sort of holy text which you have to thoroughly study from beginning to end. By *assessing and selecting* you have taken control with a positive, and not a passive, approach. After assessment, if you do decide you need to read and note most of a chapter this is an effective method.

Extracting Ideas and Information from a Chapter

The worst way you can approach a chapter of, say, 15 pages is to start to read and note from the first page and plod through to the finish. In a manner similar to your response to the book as a whole, first survey the chapter. Flick through the pages and paragraphs to see the sequence of subjects and the analysis or argument. These may be indicated in the first, or sometimes the last, sentence of the paragraph. As you skim through, your eye will catch sight of evidence - events and dates. If you're an average student, and most students are, and careful with your reading, you will normally read slowly. To skim a chapter you will need to *force your eyes* to read in a different way, almost a casual way. You may not be good at this at first but the more you try and practise the more expert you will become. Just as we walk in different ways, we stroll, amble down a high street, go for a hike for several hours or rush to catch a bus, and yet we walk in every instance, so the effective student will have different styles of reading and choose an appropriate style for a particular task. The one style, one speed, reader undertakes study with a major handicap.

SQ3R - A Formula for Effective Reading

You have now *Surveyed* the chapter and completed the first stage of the classic formula for reading and noting, SQ3R. The second part,

Q for *question*, reminds you to prepare your mind to be active: in this you should question what your skim reading has suggested the pages present and what *you* want from them. It is helpful, also, to notice and question the writer's interpretation and argument. You decide what is needed for *your* purpose. Just because the writer covers certain topics it does not mean that you have to read and note them. Only do so if it serves your study purpose. Next, the 3 Rs. They represent *Read, Recall* and *Report.* This is the stage for more careful reading, remembering (recalling) what you read followed by a report, that is the notes of what you decide to write (from memory). Always try to use *your own words* when you write notes. If you are new to this effective procedure it is best to be realistic: you will not read, recall and report more than two or three pages at a time until you become more skilled. When you first try higher-skill reading you will not be very quick but your speed will increase as you practise. The SQ3R procedure may seem complicated but students who gain most from a unit of time and effort use it.

Reasons for Notemaking and the Depth of Notes

Noting is arguably one of the most tedious aspects of study. So why make notes? There are two main reasons. First, to help you understand a passage from a history book, its contents, structure and argument and, second, to provide a permanent record of the book's information and ideas - a record that can be used for essays and for exams in months' or years' time. Both the first and second reasons mean the layout of your notes is very important. There are a few guidelines which, if you follow them, will greatly increase the value of your notes.

Before these are outlined there is an important question to consider. How detailed a record of your reading should your notes be? The answer is not straightforward because the detail will depend on the purpose of your reading. If you read to gain the main argument or themes from a chapter, your notes will be only your summary of the argument or themes. If, on the other hand, you are reading the chapter of a textbook in order to gain a thorough outline of a topic which you have not previously studied, you will want to make more comprehensive notes.

Whichever type of notemaking you choose, you need to note at the appropriate depth and thoroughness. There are two errors to avoid: notes which are too skimpy and notes which are too detailed and too thorough. The first impedes revision and learning, the second requires too much effort and might obstruct your grasp of the topic as a whole and slow your information search. The best notes are those which are just on the edge of being too thin, that is too short. If they fall below the level of being clear, because they are too short, all is not lost - see the final point of the next section on layout (page 12).

The Layout of Your Notes

The two reasons for notes are to help your understanding and to provide a record to enable you to revise and learn the topic. These two reasons are a guide to the layout of notes. Notes are more helpful when not written like a book, with paragraphs made up of sentences. They should be items of information or ideas or steps in an argument or analysis. When you come to revise or learn your topic you should not need to study the pages to sort out information. Good notes can be learned by rapid scanning. To make this possible the layout is very important.

Here are a few features good note layout will have:

- Headings and subheadings, which are presented in such a way that the reader's eye is drawn to them because they are written in larger letters or underlined or highlighted in some way.
- There is no need to write in complete sentences. Notes are not the place to improve your expression and grammar.
- Use contractions for frequently used words to save time and effort. Work out contractions that are useful to you. Your notes are only for you: they don't need to be understood by other people. A few contractions which are commonly used include: The first letter of the name often written (G for Gladstone); v instead of against; an arrow to show 'leads to', and so on.
- While it is important to have a meaningful layout, your handwriting needs only to be legible for you. Don't waste time with immaculate handwriting.
- Space out your notes. White space on a page is a quick indicator of note quality: leave a lot of it. If you are successful with good layout this will happen anyway. There is no need to worry about the paper cost of spaced-out notes: the additional cost of paper is minimal, equivalent to one drink in your college bar a term.
- Well laid out notes have graded indentation (the position of the start of words from the left margin) to present the structure and indicate the importance and relationship of information.

The Church in 1529

Emergence of a Nation State by AGR Smith pp 13 – 17
(1984)

p13   Four features of the Church in 1529

- wealth
- unpopularity (anticlericalism) with laymen
- challenge from reform movements outside the (Roman)
    church
    - Lollards
    - Lutherans
- the Church's dependence, in England, on the Crown

WEALTH

Its lands worth about £370,000 pa (rents)
    - about half went to monasteries
    - about half to secular clergy (in parishes)
     i.e. about 20% of England's land owned
      by the church

Signs of its wealth, its buildings : cathedrals, churches
     and monasteries gold and silver
     plate, artistic treasures

ANTICLERICALISM

why?
1. wealth, made worse by Wolsey's lifestyle and
    love of splendour
2. standards of the clergy: they were as good as
    before BUT expectations were higher
3. irritations, especially ecclesiastical courts
     pluralism
      tithes
    The Hunne case, 1511-14 showed these
    irritations.
    Hunne case led to dispute in Parliament
    over benefit of clergy

   This anticlericalism still evident in the early
   sessions of the Reformation Parliament.
p14   AGRS calls this type of anticlericalism
   'negative anticlericalism.'

Figure 1. The layout of your notes: imposing structure. Indentation, white space and subheadings in capitals are used to add structure and indicate importance. Notice that the source is recorded at the top as well as the pages from which the notes are made. Page references are added in the margin to enable rapid location of the information in the text, if needed.

The Layout of Your Notes   **11**

- Impose structure on your notes so that importance is shown and dependent, supporting information is indicated by your layout.
- All notes should be headed by the full title of the book from which they are made, the author, date of publication and, if the book is from a library, the class mark. Further, in the left-hand margin of your notes, add the page number of the book on which the notes are made fairly frequently. This good practice takes no time to do but it can save you hours if your notes are not overfull and you need to check something at the time of revision.

Notes from Lectures

Lecture styles differ so widely that suggestions on making notes is difficult. Nevertheless, a few general comments can be made. Two main reasons for making notes in lectures is to help your concentration and to summarise the themes or arguments of the lecturer. There are two types of notes made in lectures which are unhelpful. First, notes where the student has attempted to record everything (the notes are too full, the arguments, analysis, themes tend to be lost in the bulk of writing) and second, notes which contain too little. It is, therefore, a matter of judgement and balance. You are unlikely to be drawn to write too much if you have completed some overview reading of the topic and so you are free to pick the main points, the structure of argument or analysis, and the telling evidence from the lecture. Lecture notes are best presented on the page with a spaced out layout and with a structure. Tape recordings of lectures do not match good notes.

Once made, it is good practice to spend 10 minutes, within the following three days, reading over your lecture notes. Time spent then, when you can still remember some of the lecture and are able to amend your notes, can save an hour of puzzlement at the end of the year.

Key points
- Decide what you need to read and read selectively.
- See texts as sources from which to extract information and analysis
- Read intelligently by use of the SQ3R procedure.
- Remember the purpose for notes. Pitch the content and layout with that in mind.

2 Hunting for Information

READING FOR AN ESSAY or assignment is, it would seem, an activity very unlike ancient villagers hunting a mammoth or an Eskimo searching arctic ice for seals, but you should recognise some similarities by the end of this chapter.

The Use of Reading Lists

Students usually begin work for an undergraduate essay with a list of sources from their tutor. If the reading list includes comments on the sources the list is a lot more helpful, but either way the list is usually students' initial information, but it is only the beginning. The list should be subjected to a number of questions which relate to *your* needs. Are all the sources necessary for you? Are the sources easily available? Are they of the same type? Should some sources be used before others? Are all the sources equally helpful? Are there other, more helpful, sources not listed? When considering these questions, have the categorisation of sources given below in mind.

The Hierarchy of Texts

If you look at a library History shelf you will see a range of types of books. This is one categorisation - but you can make your own.
- Short summary reviews, 100 to 150 pages, such as Lancaster Pamphlets or Macmillan - Studies in European History series.
- Students' basic texts of narrative and analysis, such as Hodder - Access to History series, Longman - Seminar Studies, Manchester University Press - New Frontiers in History series or Routledge - Historical Connections series.
- Major texts, often in a series, which thoroughly cover several aspects of history over, say, 80 years - for example Longman's Foundations of Modern Britain or the Short Oxford History of the Modern World.
- Texts which bring together work on particular themes, sometimes in series, for example Macmillan's Social History in Perspective

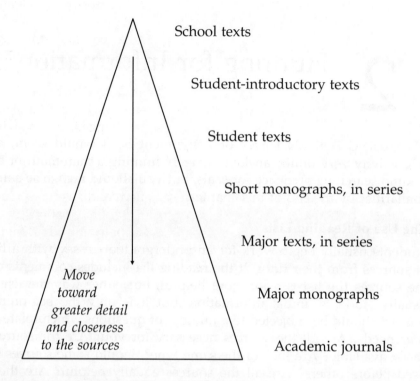

School texts

Student-introductory texts

Student texts

Short monographs, in series

Major texts, in series

Move toward greater detail and closeness to the sources

Major monographs

Academic journals

Figure 2. Stylised diagram of the hierarchy of texts

series or texts, such as Longman's Profiles in Power series, assembled round a person or collections of essays on a topic, such as Macmillan's Problems in Focus series.

- The next step in thoroughness and complexity can be represented by major works on a particular topic: for example J.J. Scarisbrick's *Henry VIII* (1968) or John Röhl's *The Kaiser and His Court* (1995).

There is a similar hierarchy for History journals. They range from shorter student-centred articles in *new perspective, History Review, Modern History Review* and *History Today* through *History, Transactions of the Royal Historical Society*, the *Historical Journal, English History Review, Past and Present* to journals, such as *Economic History Review, Ecclesiastical History, European Review of History* and *The Local Historian*, which serve subdisciplines of History.

Stage 1: An Appropriate Point of Entry

The point to be made is that, depending on how well you know the topic because of previous work, you should enter the information chain (the hierarchy of information) at the appropriate level and avoid the temptation to enter at too high a level.

For the sake of argument, let us assume that you know nothing about the topic. What is the best strategy to follow when you have access to a rich array of books and journals? As the topic is new to you, your first task is to gain a general overview which will give you some perspective over the whole topic. Once you have an overall view you will be less likely to be bogged down with information, the significance of which will be unclear to you, and your subsequent reading will be more meaningful. Therefore, find a short summary or general account to read first. At this stage your notes should be general rather than detailed and, as you read, reference to a chronology or, better still, your creation of a chronology (on a separate piece of paper) will help you to orientate yourself. You may find a short summary or general account in a Lancaster Pamphlet, Hodder - Access to History or a Longman - Seminar Studies type book. If you cannot find a short summary then a good encyclopaedia account would be better than nothing.

In addition to your short notes and a chronology, a list of questions, to which you will later seek answers (write them, either at the bottom of your pages as you write notes or on a separate sheet) is even more useful, because it will prime your mind to search for what you need to deepen your understanding.

Stage 2: Further Steps towards Topic Mastery

Having gained a foundation of understanding, you are ready for the next stage of research into your topic. This stage will require you to consider the books from your tutor's list and books listed in bibliographies at the end of the shorter studies. Bibliographies which include comments about the books are particularly helpful. At this second stage you will probably use two kinds of books. You will read chapters, or parts of chapters, of major texts and monographs (books on only one subject). Your notes, at this second stage, will be more selective but more thorough.

Stage 3: Adding Scholarly Refinement

When you have both an overview and a good grounding on the topic, stages 1 and 2, your final stage or work could be to search out books or articles which are particularly sharp or controversial in their interpretation and analysis, and books which give powerful insights. Examples of the latter could be Friedrich Meinecke's *The*

German Catastrophe, Carlo Ginzburg's *The Cheese and the Worms* or Fritz Fischer's *Germany's War Aims in the First World War,* and these books, which can add greatly to your understanding, are not necessarily huge in size. You should see yourself as a sort of Inspector Morse and develop a dectective's 'nose' for really helpful books. You can gain some idea which these are especially from repeated references in the books you read, from footnotes and from comments in bibliographies. (Whether you share these finds with your friends, it is not for me to say!) Academic journal articles, usually focused on a theme or argument, summarise recent research or new interpretations. They can be dense and turgid but the skilful reader will speedily extract the key ideas and evidence. Higher-level texts usually have references which lead you to articles. Use of this type of information will convey to your tutor that you are an experienced and capable information and interpretation acquirer and that you have begun to make inroads into the mastery of the topic.

The three-stage strategy outlined here is a simplification of the procedure a skilled student will follow. In practice, you will probably work on stage 3 while continuing with stage 2.

Time for Securing Sources

Alert students find the most important resources quickly. You may find the best books which you want to consult are not available until your assignment is finished because smarter students, who are more organised and quicker, take out the texts before you.

Key points

- Begin from the short, general accounts in order to gain an overview.
- Decide which sources to proceed to next. These books will be the books which are right for *you* because they relate to questions *you* want to find answers to as you read.
- Time and effort will be needed to find these books. They will not arrive, unsolicited in plain brown packages, in your room.
- Seek out sources which are particularly illuminating. They may be monographs or articles in academic journals. Use them carefully and selectively to add refinement to your work.
- When you are familiar with the topic, seek out sources which give sharp interpretations, theories and arguments.

16   Time for Securing Sources

3 Working on Information

HABITS OF WORK can be likened to explosives: they can be beneficial (the clearance of slums to enable the construction of beautiful buildings) or harmful (the destruction of people by bombs or bullets). One habit of study which undergraduate History students can slip into is very unbeneficial. If you have this bad habit you may have carried it over from school History. Under pressure to complete topics and meet essay deadlines, it is easy to allow work procedure to have only two parts: reading with noting and essay writing. This is a reduced procedure and encourages a 'cut and paste' approach to essays and leads to lower grades. With the middle stage of work omitted, working on information, a downward spiral of low achievement and motivation can begin.

The Middle Stage in Study: Adding Value to Time and Effort

Good readers and note makers will be *active* thinkers and not passive copiers of information (Chapter 1). Students with even rudimentary skills will process their information before an essay answer is written (Chapter 7). Better students will do more because the middle stage between reading/noting and essay writing has the potential to be the greatest 'value added' activity for students. It adds to your interest and it enables you to increase your understanding of the topic and to gain more reward for the time given to study.

Middle Stage Activity for Greater Understanding

This middle stage work on information can take many forms.
- At its simplest, it should include the creation of a chronology for summary or content, fashioned for your purpose, if this was not undertaken during reading (figure 3).
- Spray diagrams or ideas maps of the main influences underneath the surface of events (figure 4). These diagrams are particularly useful because they depict the relationship between events. These

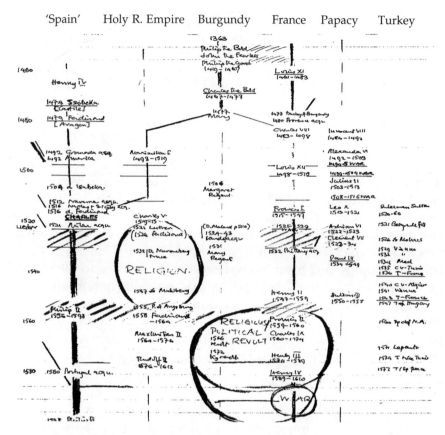

Figure 3. Illustration of a chronology of European history, 1440-1600, which summarises key developments, draws out inter-state relations and major features (linear and lateral) of the period

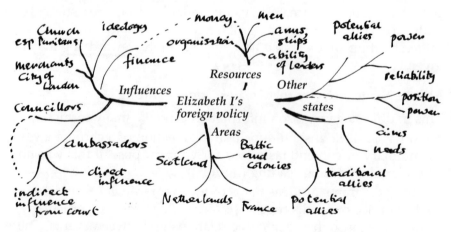

Figure 4. Spray diagram of Elizabeth I's foreign policy

18   Middle Stage Activity for Greater Understanding

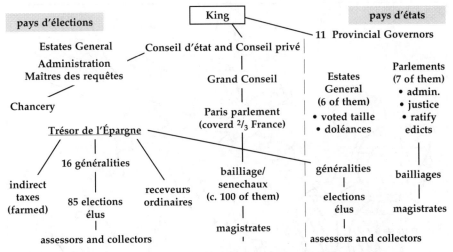

Figure 5. Early-modern French government structure, clarifies text descriptions

influences are what scientists call variables. I shall refer to them again later in 'mind games and counterfactuals', page 21.

- Government structure sketches, if they are not provided in texts, will clarify your reading (figure 5).
- Placement of the history within the contemporary social, economic and political structure. You may find it useful to create your own diagram (figure 6).
- Reference to maps can help you understand why events could occur as they did: atlases, even if not historical atlases, are a neglected aid to understanding. A sketch map of the main place

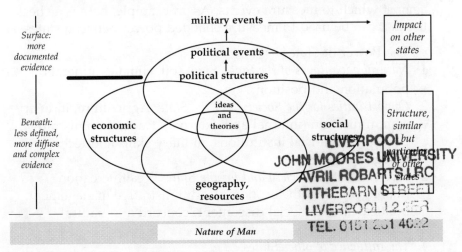

Figure 6. Diagram of the relationship of events and underlying structures

Middle Stage Activity for Greater Understanding **19**

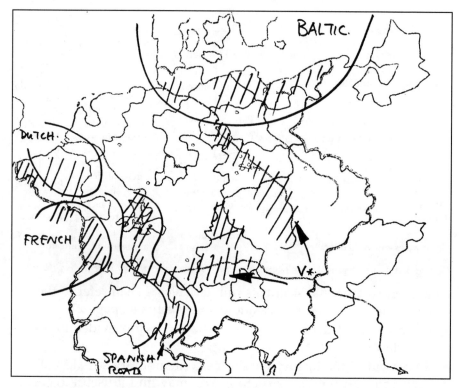

Figure 7. Sketch map of the areas of fighting during the Thirty Years' War

of activity can bring out patterns which you had not noticed in a
textbook (see the map of the Thirty Years' War, figure 7).

- Development of check lists for analysis. These are headings
  against which to measure events. As an example, here is a check
  list that can be used to measure changed power between states.

  The Power of States
  1 *Natural advantages of the State.* Size, soil, climate, minerals,
    population and position.
  2 *Opportunities for the Society and the State.* Agriculture, industry,
    communication (internal and external), trade, administrative,
    fiscal and financial institutions, military skills and tech-
    nological innovation.
  3 *Problems within Society and for the State.* Wealth creation
    (management of the economy), administrative management,
    political and/or social discontent/concord and natural
    disasters.
  4 *The Influence of other States.*

Mind Games and Counterfactuals

Games you can play with historical information are senseless in one way. After all, no one can change what actually happened. In another way they can help the student toward a more full understanding. Historians tend not to play mind games in public but there are examples, including Geoffrey Parker's 'If the Armada had Landed' (*History*, October 1976) and Jeremy Black's 'Could Bonnie Prince Charlie have Won?' (*History Today*, July 1995). Here are four kinds of mind games you can play.

- Isolate the main elements in a historical situation. Now vary one of the elements and see how the others are affected. Try this with the reasons for Spanish decline in the seventeenth century (figure 8).

- Change the order of events and assess the probable consequences. This is especially useful if events changed greatly within a short space of time. Example: Russia's acceptance of negotiations with Austria on 1 August 1914 after the German decision for war on Russia. Exchange the order. Is it possible subsequent events could have been different?

- Remove one or two juxtapositioned events and estimate the possible direction of events. Example: remove the expulsion of the 'Sea Beggars' from Dover (in 1572) from the Dutch revolt.

- Assume that some important project/aim that succeeded had failed (or that failed, had succeeded). Assess the consequences. Examples: Thomas Wyatt's rising led to the capture of London,

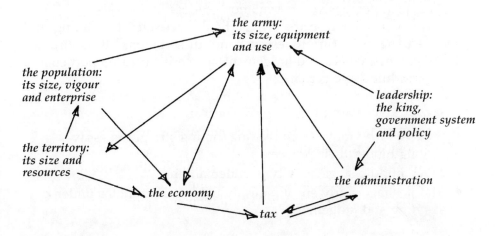

Figure 8. The influences on Spanish power in the seventeenth century

1554, or Cavour failed to make an agreement with Napoleon III in 1859.

This middle phase of work, between reading/noting and essay writing can increase understanding and is not as demanding as the first or third stages of work. It does not require long periods of uninterrupted time. Some of this kind of activity can be fitted in while waiting for something to start, say a lecture, and middle-stage work can seem little more than doodling but, because your mind is active and the information is considered, sorted, filtered and reworked, your understanding is enhanced.

The Middle Stage and the Development of Judgement

Students often choose to study History as undergraduates either because they are good at it or because they enjoy the subject, or both. Whatever the reason, a History degree will open the door to many careers (see Chapter 18). Very few of these careers require the use of the knowledge graduates had gained as History students. Would not a course with a strong vocational content, say, Media Studies, Business Studies, Law and so on, be better? The answer is that the subject matter of History may not be directly relevant to graduate careers but because History students develop transferable skills it is, indirectly, very relevant. With *transferable* skills, History graduates have more flexibility than, say, a Law graduate. Under-graduate History study fosters (i) the development of skills for absorbing and using a lot of information, (ii) the development of skills of analysis and judgement and (iii) the development of the skill of clear, persuasive, presentation of ideas in answers.

You will recognise that (i) particularly relates to reading and note making and (iii) to essays and dissertations. It is (ii), the development analysis and judgement, which is nurtured particularly during middle-stage activity.

Key points
- Students who move from reading/noting straight to essay writing hinder their progress.
- Much middle-stage activity is undemanding.
- Middle-stage study encourages thought and promotes under-standing and judgement.

4 Talking and Listening

WHILE STRUGGLING with the question of how a society may be justly governed, the eighteenth-century French writer Jean Jacques Rousseau, whose thought contributed to the dissatisfaction which formed the French Revolution, wrote what was later published as *The Social Contract* (1762). In those brief pages he powerfully provided the reasons for our preference to live together in groups, in society, a course which is chosen by all but a very few of us. Only a handful of individuals, such as Julian of Norwich, choose a life of contemplative solitude.

News about people and events is part of the glue of social life. The Media, apart from its role in a political audit, helps meet this need. That is why people so regularly update on news and on gossip column content, although reports in *Sunday Sport* that Hitler escaped from the Berlin bunker and travelled to Mars in a B52 bomber and that a correspondent's friend was eaten by a brussels sprout belong to comical fiction. And students, when they are not lectured to or participate in tutorials and seminars, readily resort to what some call gossip and some call chat, and few would question that in general gossip and chat, about sport or relationships or whatever, is wholesome.

Turning Talking and Listening to Advantage

The work-obsessive undergraduate (which is not a theme of this book) is not attractive but talking and listening about the subject of your study will help you make large strides towards higher-grade work.

The aspect of talking and listening emphasised now is not the tutorial but talking and listening between friends and colleagues, anyone with whom you share the course and with whom you have some rapport. You may meet her/him because you are in the same hall of residence, in the same sports team or because you made an acquaintance through a tutorial or in a coffee bar.

Your tasks as an undergraduate include the absorption of much

Turning Talking and Listening to Advantage

information. At the end, the extent of your success as a History student is assessed (apart from presentations) by what you write - in essay, dissertation or exam. In between, information has to be assessed, ordered, analysed, ideas tested and judgements made. In Chapter 3 (Working on Information) I suggested some activities for this middle stage of work. Talking and listening is another.

Discussions with fellow students, sometimes almost casual and sometimes brief, sometimes more protracted, in which your ideas are put into words and explained, your theories, assessments and judgements are tested against the critically constructive response of the listener, will help to clarify and shape your thought and sharpen and improve expression. We can think in our head and get away with muddle but once words are spoken dodgy thought, incoherence and nonsense is audible.

You spend a good deal of time as a student as a receiver of information and ideas from books and lectures. The main time you deliver, not receive, is when you write course and exam essays. So there is an imbalance between 'taking in' and 'giving out'. Discussion is one way to increase the 'giving out', but it requires a lot less effort than essay writing. Even if informal discussion does not require the precision and rigour of essay work, it does further clarity of thought and understanding.

Of course, most discussion between two students will have a rough balance between talking and listening, but in any case the listener is not a loser. The listener has the opportunity to hear the other students' views and ideas, ideas to which they will probably readily relate, and listening and seeking to see sense in what is said will further the listener's own familiarity with the topic, help towards their own sorting out and improve their own clarity of thought. Above all, discussion adds energy and interest for your work.

Talking and Listening in Tutorials and Seminars

Tutorials and seminars are a forum for talking and listening in a formal setting. The worst tutorials are those in which students sit in awkward silence while the poor old tutor, poor because the government has not increased salaries in real terms since 1986 and old in comparison with students, gamely tries to engender discussion.

To benefit from tutorials you need to have some grounding in the topic. This you will have if you have completed at least your preliminary reading (see pages 14 and 15) and thereby have a foundation for discussion. After that, the success of the tutorial (for you) will depend on your (and other students') willingness to contribute. Students with bottle and verve are not overawed by tutors and other students. Tutorials can be especially useful because, although the most tedious side of study is the acquisition of information by reading, the most helpful/valuable side is the ideas, theories and arguments, and the tutorial is an occasion when these are raised and discussed. Even an incorrect theory or a flawed argument, in so far as it encourages you to think and discuss, is useful to you and your tutorial members. That is why all can contribute once they have a grounding on a topic. If you discuss your ideas with your friends, as recommended earlier in this chapter, you will find it easier to contribute to tutorials and you will gain more from them. Of course, an argument, in discussion or in an essay, is only as good as the evidence upon which it is based and the soundness of the reasoning used.

Key points
- Talking with friends, even in a casual way, about the topics you study, should not be neglected.
- Talking is an easy and enjoyable way to help sort out information, test judgements and assessments and further clarity of thought and expression.
- Tutorials provide an opportunity to hear ideas and to test arguments in a more formal setting.
- In discussion, informal or formal, the listener also benefits.

5 People and Historical Study

THERE IS AN INTENTIONAL AMBIGUITY in the title of this chapter. 'People and Historical Study' can refer to persons who lived in the past and were therefore part of history. On the other hand the title can mean persons, such as you, who study the past. In both senses people are central in historical study. As I will show in the latter part of the chapter, these two but different meanings are linked.

People in the Past

Most History studied before the undergraduate years is strong in political themes. I accept that there are economic and social History courses but most school students follow a course centred on politics, politicians, power, states and foreign policies. During the under-graduate years there is more diversity in subject options and student choice. Many undergraduates, for example, as part of their course, follow gender studies, cultural History, diplomatic or racial History themes. Whatever the theme of the chosen course, people remain at the centre of the subject.

While films, CD-Roms, pictures or material remains (buildings, artefacts …) may add to our appreciation of the past, the written word, in the form of books, articles and documents, remain the dominant way into the past. Information in books, that is by the written word, presents a danger and a challenge, but the challenge provides an opportunity. The danger is that you will let the past you study remain a 'book past'. That is, that you allow an account of the events of the past, made from the lives of people and their actions, remain detached from you on the written page in the book before you. The challenge of the written past is to transfer it from the pages to inside your head where you make it a *living* past, in which a cast of people as real as family and friends, who you can be with in your mind, even when they are not with you in the same room or building. If you make some progress towards capturing the past in this way your interest, understanding and enjoyment, as well as

Figure 9. People in History

your insights and mastery, will markedly advance.

The key to unlock the life of the past, so that it lives in your mind, is to search for the people in the past. Decisions are made by people, implemented by people and effect the lives of people. Wars are made by people, mostly men, and are fought by men and women. Civilians' lives are changed by war: civilians are people just as your neighbours and friends are people. Even 'dry' administrative History is the result of decisions which, when implemented, influence people. People are party to every aspect of History. They provide a handle for us, in the present, because people are the constant in History. While economics and societies change, landscapes are transformed, nations become stronger or weaker, the people in these histories are substantially the same as you and me. They have the same needs, the same range of emotions and capacity for virtue and vice. It is your direct access to human nature that can go direct to the heart of the real past - the lives of people and the events in which they had a part.

The Past, People and the Present

I now refer to the other meaning of the chapter title. If you accept my central positioning of people in History and the importance of the incorporation of past lives in students' minds to enliven the past, how can this be done with most effect? Let us liken History, that is either the past or an account of the past in a History book, to a work of art, say a Henry Moore statue, or to a novel. It is unlikely that two people will respond to the statue or to a novel in exactly the same way. The statue or novel, however, is the same entity so if the response is not the same it is because the responders, the viewers or readers, are different. In short, any communication has three steps - a communicator, a communication and a communication receiver. If History, whether the past or an account of the past, is set then the extent of appreciation to that set History will vary dependent on the responder - the History student or historian. The more you move toward a fuller understanding of yourself and people in the present, the more you will understand the people of the past and therefore the past itself. The value of the present to help with the study of the past is implied by Marc Bloch's comment: 'This solidarity of the ages is so effective that the lines of communication work both ways. ... a man may wear himself out ... in seeking to understand the past, if he is totally ignorant of the present. ... This faculty of understanding the living is, in very truth, the master quality of the historian.' (*The Historian's Craft*, English edition 1954.) And how can your understanding of yourself be more full? By living a busy, rounded, challenging life and by a developing self awareness and curiosity about people and society and how institutions really work *today*. For these insights, gained from an interest in the present, which is more accessible, and more fully reported, and which is more open to immediate questioning than the past, is a really useful way towards an understanding of the people of the past.

A further turn in the relationship of past, present and people is the role of the past to help our understanding of the present and ourselves, a theme which is not explored here. The past, present and people can be seen as apexes in a triangle in which each furthers comprehension of the other two.

Key points
- To bring energy and interest to your study of the past, think of the people in the past as just as real as the people you know in the present.
- As you 'see' beyond the surface on events in the present, and as you gain more awareness of the possibilities of human nature, both yours and other people's, so your apprecation of the past increases.

6 History Analysis

A S YOU PROGRESSED with your earlier study of History the approach to the subject changed, bit by bit, from mostly narrative History, the story of history, to more and more analysis. In other words, there was a change from answering the questions What? Who? and When? to How? and Why? And in the latter years of your school History course your teachers probably commented that better students gain higher grades because they analyse their topics.

What is Analysis?

Analysis refers to the breakdown of a complicated whole, such as a passage of History, into smaller parts and the identification of influences and the relationship of the parts to each other.

What is analysis? Consider the picture of the clock (below). If we liken the hour and minute hands to the movements of history, that is the changing events, to understand those changing events we need to identify the reasons for the changes. In the case of the clock

Figure 10. Defining analysis: a clock face and mechanism

What is Analysis?

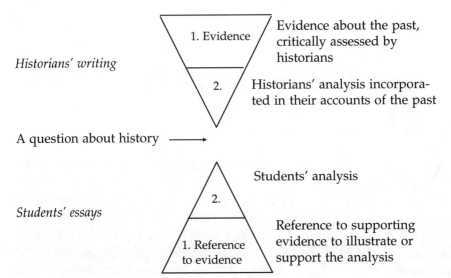

Historians' writing

1. Evidence

Evidence about the past, critically assessed by historians

2.

Historians' analysis incorporated in their accounts of the past

A question about history ⟶

Students' essays

Students' analysis

2.

1. Reference to evidence

Reference to supporting evidence to illustrate or support the analysis

Figure 11. Analysis in History books and students' essays

the reasons include the cogs and their positional relationship to each other as well as the spring, which provides the mechanical force. An alert, investigatory student of History is not satisfied with finding out only the position of the hands, what? of history, but will penetrate below the surface of events to give answers to the question why?

The reasons for events are often not explicit and evidential (that is, there is often no hard evidence for events) but circumstantial; the reason is inferred by the circumstances of the events. Consider an example from the world of physics: if you hold an apple in your hand at waist height and then release your grip, the apple falls to the ground. The fall of the apple is an event in history and you can answer a 'what' question: the apple fell to the ground. The 'why' question will be answered by giving the reasons; the influences and forces involved. You ended the force of your grip on the apple and the force of gravity was the influence for the apple to move to the ground.

Analysis in Books and Analysis in Essays

Writers of History books start with the evidence of events but a book which was a summary of evidence would be little more than a chronicle. Books provide an analysis but the narrative and analysis are mixed together. History books can be represented as an inverted triangle (figure 11).

When you answer an essay question your answer should go in the opposite direction: you should produce an analysis of the subject in answer to the question and add the evidence to support your analysis. There is further discussion of essay preparation in the next chapter.

If history analysis is expected from you as an undergraduate and is important, how can you go about this task? You will find historians' analyses in their books but it is even better to provide your own, although you will use their analyses as a starting point.

Most of the suggestions in Chapter 3, Working on Information, will help you towards your own analysis. My late colleague, Michael Barlen, devised a method which developed students' capacity for analysis which can be called the 'Factors and Phases Method'. In this he took an identified passage of History, for

PHASES / FACTORS	1 The nobles revolt	2 Calvin-ist rising	3 Rebels gain a base	4 Divi-sions harden	5 Spanish power revival	6 Spanish diver-sions	7 Maurice consoli-dates
Date	1560-2	1566-8	1572-6	1576-9	1583-6	1586-93	1593-07
a. Social groups involved							
b. Issues - on both sides							
c. Leaders on both sides							
d. Political or military action							
e. Military events - land or sea							
f. Role of religion							
g. Third power involvement							
h. Spanish/rebel resources							
j. Spanish priorities							

Figure 12. The Factors and Phases Method with the Dutch revolt, 1560-1607

Analysis in Books and Analysis in Essays

example the Dutch Revolt, 1560-1607. From the narrative of events the phases of the revolt are decided. They can be identified by changes in the place or nature of the conflict. Phases for a topic are usually fairly clear but if you choose unusual phases the method is not invalidated. Next, the factors are decided, the contributory influences, aspects or components of the revolt. Taking the phases as a horizontal axis and the factors as the vertical axis you have created a grid. Summary information (from your notes) entered in the grid boxes will indicate the dynamic, the pattern and the relationships between events. It is accepted that this method can distort and simplify the past (and reductionism lowers the quality of historical study) but work with factors and phases will engage your mind, bring out connections, help understanding and make essay writing far easier. There is a fuller discussion of Factors and Phases Method in *The Good History Students' Handbook*, Chapter 7, pp. 52-60.

There is no pretence that factors and phases analysis provides a final and definitive analysis of a topic but it is a procedure to help you towards a fuller understanding and a help for you to think for yourself. You are not expected, in your undergraduate work, to write the final truth of History. The primary purpose, as an undergraduate, is to develop your intellectual capacity (see Chapter 18). As a student you are not expected to pretend you are a research historian but indications of your own thought, judgement and analysis in your essay answers (which are considered in the next chapter), as long as they are not wildly implausible, will be valued and rewarded.

Key points
- Analysis is a powerful intellectual skill.
- Analysis is the breakdown of a complicated whole and the identification of the influences and relationship of the parts.
- Students are not required to produce definitive History. Their development of the capacity for analysis, because it indicates thought, will be given credit.

7 Writing Essays

ESSAYS, whether for coursework or exams, are a major part of undergraduate work and they require sharply defined skills which all students are able to develop and master. Students begin their undergraduate studies with different levels of essay writing expertise and, therefore, my comments are divided into two: basic procedures and advanced essay writing. Your tutors will inform you of the number of words required and the system for referencing sources.

The Question

An essay is your response to a particular question and your tutors and examiners expect you to direct all you write to that particular question. Sometimes students' essays are admirable in every respect except for the failure to answer the question: they receive less reward, therefore, than they otherwise deserve so it is prudent to consider the question with care.

To be clear what the question asks, try this procedure. Underline the key words and re-write the question in your own words. You will notice that most questions at your level require analysis or judgement of the topic you have studied. If you have undertaken some of the suggestions in Chapter 3 and Chapter 6 essay preparation will be easier.

Essay Preparation

- First, with the question clear in your mind look over your notes and, also, what you produced during the 'working with information' and 'analysis' stages. Write on a rough piece of paper information and ideas that relate to the question.

- Second, when you have finished looking over your notes, consider all the information and ideas, which were relevant to the question, which you scribbled down. From these rough notes you will probably find an overall theme or argument. This will become the centre of your answer to the question. (If you don't find a theme or argument search your notes again.)

- Third, with your theme or argument decided, arrange your scribbled information and ideas into points which support your theme or argument. Each of these points will be stages in your essay, with a paragraph each, in support of your theme or argument.

- Fourth, now place in order these supporting arguments with the most important first and the least important last. This arrangement will enable you to present your most powerful case in support of your theme or argument.

When you are planning an answer, especially in an exam, it is useful to have a headings' check list so that, instead of waiting to stumble across information and ideas, you have reference points to what could be relevant. You can make your own check lists. Here is one, designed to be memorised easily, for early-modern English History:

Government.	King. Council. Committees. Court.
Administration.	Chancery. Exchequer. Courts, London and Assize. Army and Navy.
Church.	Bishops. Convocation. Priests. Orders.
Policy.	Foreign. Fiscal. Religious. Economic. Social.
Functions.	King: Law. Defence. Order. Patronage. Oversee administration.
	Subjects: Loyalty. Help - advice and military aid and Money.

With your rough working finished you have thought through the question and your answer and you have prepared your essay plan. With this thinking completed, and your sketch plan made, you are free to concentrate on writing your answer as clearly and as persuasively as possible.

Essay Structure

The emphasis of undergraduate essay work is on argument. High-grade essays have a very clear structure, which enables the reader to follow easily the argument. Summarise your argument or main theme in your introduction - thereby you make it clear to the reader the direction of your answer. Your introduction, which is, of course, the summary of your full essay, is best if it is short (just a

34

Essay Preparation

The Question

Read the question with care

Underline the key words

See the meaning of the question

In Rough

Write ideas and supporting evidence (people, events, dates ...) relevant to the question

Review your jottings and order your rough notes

Decide on an overall summary of your arguments

Write

Write your summary in the introduction

Write no more than one idea/argument (with supporting evidence) in each paragraph

Write your argument / judgement / idea as the first sentence of each paragraph

Take care to express yourself with clarity

If you have time - read, check and correct your answer

Figure 13. The essay preparation memo sheet. When asked to identify the most helpful study skills sheet students often choose this one

few lines in length) because, thereby, your argument will be more clear, if not mixed with other information. Your second, third, fourth ... paragraphs support your main theme or argument.

Aim to write the main point of each paragraph as the first sentence. The first sentence of each paragraph, therefore, defines the content of the paragraph. The rest of the paragraph should be a reference to events which illustrate, support or explain the main point of your paragraph.

The short essay answer example (partially in note form) on pages 37-8 illustrates clearly the procedure. You will note from this example that the essay has only three elements: 1) The summary of the answer which is written in the introduction; 2) Four statements, written at the beginning of the subsequent paragraphs, to support the summary. The third element, in the four paragraphs after the introduction, is *reference* to events which support or illustrate the theme of the paragraph. With the argument stated in the introduction and supported in the four paragraphs, a conclusion is not needed but it could be added as an option.

Essay Assessment

The reasons an essay prepared in this way will score well. When your essay answers are assessed the reader will use six criteria.

1. Does the essay have an argument or theme and is it directed to the question asked?
2. Is well-chosen evidence used to support or illustrate the theme or argument?
3. Is the essay structured to develop the argument?
4. Is the presentation of the argument persuasive and the English correct, clear and effective?
5. Does the essay indicate the writer has a sound understanding of the topic and its context?
6. Does the essay have indications of the writer's own thought and, where appropriate, does the essay show awareness of other views and debates on the subject?

You will note that students who follow the procedures outlined will score well with criteria 1, 2 and 3. Criterion 4 will be considered in Chapter 8 and criteria 5 and 6 will reflect, partly, your work with reading, noting and working with information. You may wish to assess the sample essay answer against the six criteria.

Question: 'The ambitions of the Borgias and Julius II were the chief cause of strife in contemporary Italy.' Discuss

Introduction

The Borgias and Julius II did contribute to the reasons for strife in Italy but they were not the only cause or even the most important. The extent of strife, the suffering of the citizens and the destruction of property during the Italian wars led Machiavelli to write *The Prince*, a masterly commentary on political behaviour.

Paragraph 2

The Borgias and Julius II (1503-1513) did help to cause fighting in Italy. The Borgias, Alexander VI (1492-1503) and Cesare, his son, who in 1498 had fought France in Italy, helped persuade Louis XII to invade in 1499: this was the second Italian war. Cesare, with the help of French troops, took from local lords most of Romagna, which he intended to be a separate Borgia state. Alexander VI died unexpectedly in 1503 to be succeeded by Popes Pius III and, in 1513, Julius II, a vigorous, secular-minded pope, who wanted to extend papal power. Julius II became, therefore, part of the League of Cambrai, 1508 (with allies France, Maximilian I of the Holy Roman Empire, and Spain joined later) against the wealthy trading republic Venice. Later, Julius II was a key member of Holy League (Spain, Venice, England and, later, Maximilian I) against France, formed in 1511. When Julius II died, in 1511, he was succeeded by the Medici, Leo X.

Paragraph 3

The Borgias and Julius II were not the only reasons for strife in Italy.

1. The first war started when, in 1494, Charles VIII of France decided to give weight to the French claim, through the illegitimate Anjou line, to the Kingdom of Naples (dated from 1484). French troops occupied Naples and there was further fighting when a league was formed against France by Ferdinand of Aragon.

2. Louis XII of France invaded in 1499 to begin the second war because his family (Orleans) had a claim to rule Milan as heirs of the Viscontis, who had been expelled by the Sforza in 1450.

3. This second war extended to Naples when Louis XII and Ferdinand agreed to partition Naples, only then to disagree and to fight one another.

4. The French suggested the League of Cambrai against Venice in 1508 and they did most of the fighting. Later, it was the Spanish who occupied Florence and Milan.

5. In 1515, the newly ascended Francis I of France, retook Milan.

Essay Example   **37**

Paragraph 4

<u>Not only were the Borgias and Julius II not the only cause, they were not the most important.</u>

    1. The part of Alexander VI in the first war, 1494-5, was minimal and he did not instigate it.

    2. Although they were involved in the second war, 1499-1504, in Romagna, the fighting there was less important than the fighting in Milan and Naples. It must, however, be accepted that Cesare Borgia encouraged Louis XII to invade, but:

    3. Louis XII of France needed no persuasion to invade Milan (in 1499);

    4. Although Julius participated in the League of Cambrai he did not initiate it. He was, however, the key figure in the Holy League against France, 1511.

Paragraph 5

Not only were the two popes not initiators of war (with the exception of the Holy League, 1511), only participants, but <u>all the aforementioned reasons for war are less important than more deep-seated reasons for the fighting</u>. These included:

    1. The end of Italian unity in 1492 (that is, the co-operation of Milan, Florence and Naples) and Sforza encouragement of France to invade Naples.

    2. The strength of government and finance in Castile (and Aragon) which gave Ferdinand the ability to raise an army and to follow traditional Aragonese interests in southern Italy. Ferdinand's general, Cordoba, a military innovator, made the army very effective. Likewise, the strengthening of the French state by Charles XII (1422-1461) and Louis XI (1461-1483) provided the means to go to war. In France, for example, an obligatory tax for a standing army was introduced in 1438, so that in 1494 Charles VIII had a sizeable, 6,000-strong, army which was a powerful force.

    3. The powers, France, Spain and the Holy Roman Empire, found it convenient to fight in another country, a country which was comparatively wealthy, especially the Venetian trading republic, and within which there was rivalry and strife and in which the complexity of the city states made conflict frequent.

Figure 14. Sample essay answer. The argument (underlined) is in the introduction and the four statements which expand the argument are the first sentence of the following four paragraphs. The rest of each paragraph is reference to the events which illustrate or support the claim in the first sentence. Note that the argument develops and has logical form. The information from which this answer was written was taken from The Age of Humanism and Reformation *by A.G. Dickens, pages 91-9 and background information pages 87-91*

Higher-level Essay Writing

Essays reflect your work on a topic and your thought about it. Better essays from students, nearer the end of their course, are clinical in their clarity and elegant in their delivery. When you have practised these essay preparation procedures and you are confident working with them you will be ready to develop further your essay skills.

Higher-level essay writing is a creative act in which you encapsulate your mastery and expertise with a topic and demonstrate your skills in scripting an answer. It is a personal statement and the essay can demonstrate a similar creative refinement as a master potter or sculptor. Without loss of focus, structure and argument, the highly skilled essay writer will reflect in the essay penetrative insights and a depth of understanding of how things are, the nature of man and the possibilities of life in society, whether present or past, in an elegantly expressed but intellectually controlled piece of writing of limited length. Such an answer will show a sure grasp of the subject, judgement in choice of telling examples and reflect the writer's own ideas. An essay of this quality, the singular creation of a reflective thinker, is light years away from the cut and paste efforts of the school pupil and it should be the aim of all undergraduates.

Key points

- Essays require defined skills which every student can master.
- Good essays are planned essays. They also reflect your reading and understanding.
- When you have practised essay preparation, you have the foundation for higher-level essay writing.
- Procedures developed for course-work essays, when applied in exam conditions, free you for high achievement.

8 English and Expression

The best time was two years ago in Hammersmith with a bunch of Midland prototypes looking for a drink down the high street. About fifteen of them. Short cunts with noddy haircuts and tasches. Stumpy little legs and beer guts. Looked like they should be on Emmerdale Farm shafting goats for a living. They clocked us coming the other way and took off. You could smell the shit over the petrol fumes, which is saying something in Hammersmith.

John King, *The Football Factory.* Jonathan Cape, 1996.

T HESE ARE THE LATTER SENTENCES of the first paragraph from a contemporary 'gritty' novel, and an indication of some of today's young person's street talk. Is it good English?

Jean Aitchinson, in her 1995 BBC Reith lectures, added vigour to the continuing debate on what is correct English and what is good English. Language has a power, the power to communicate, when it is in tune with the needs and usage of people. That is why acceptable grammar, the meaning of words and styles of expression, have always changed, and continue to change. How does this affect you, a student?

It is necessary for you to accept that your degree course writing should not be in anything like street talk, of which John King's novel is a strong example, but in the formal English of your academic discipline. You should not write or speak your answers in the colloquial language you speak to your friends, because that is not what is expected by those who assess your answers. However good you are as a student of History you are assessed by your written work and a refined, clear, robust English style can raise your assessment grades by up to 50 per cent. English and expression, therefore, matter a great deal. I agree that the English of scholarship, as English in general, changes and is not as it was 40 years ago but if you aim for high standards you will have an advantage. This chapter presents a few guidelines to help you.

Basics of Grammar (for most readers, just a reminder)

Sentences. Sentences contain a subject and a main verb. (Verbs are doing or being words.) A sentence is started with a capital letter and finished with a full stop. Example: Bismarck was Chancellor of Germany. Kennedy prepared a nuclear strike during the Cuban missile crisis.

A weakness of some students' answers is long, rambling sentences. If your sentences are too long, break them into shorter sentences but do not write only short sentences: try to have a mixture.

Capital letters. Capital letters are used to mark the beginning of each sentence and for the first letters of people, places, historical eras, institutions, ships and aircraft and trade names. Examples: Edward Heath; Trafalgar Square; Medieval York; House of Lords; *Titanic;* Lancaster bomber; Vauxhall Vectra. Note, that seasons and areas do not have a capital; for example, spring and southern England. As a general rule, use capital letters for a particular and a small letter for the general. Example: Britain won the Second World War but was unsuccessful in other wars.

Punctuation. The full stop. A full stop is used to mark the end of all sentences except direct questions (ended by ?) and exclamations (ended by !). History students will use these exceptions rarely. A full stop is also used with initials and after abbreviations (e.g. No. (number), a.m.). However, it is now common and acceptable to omit full stops with heavily used capital initials; for example: UN, BBC, IBM, MP.

Comma. Commas have no fixed rules for their use. They need to be used with care because their use can change the emphasis or meaning of a sentence. Commas are used to separate a clause within a sentence. A clause is part of the sentence but has a verb in it. For example: Henry VIII, who married Ann Bolyn, insisted on the breach with Rome in 1533. Commas are often used in pairs, as is illustrated in the last example. The key to the good use of the comma is to imagine you have to speak the sentence you write. Put the commas where you pause in the sentence.

Semi-colon and colon. A semi-colon marks a longer pause, a more definite break in a sentence. A colon is used to introduce something. It may be a list or an elaboration of a point made previously or it may be a quotation.

Apostrophe. The apostrophe indicates the possession of a thing or a quality by someone or something. For example: The machine

Basics of Grammar

gun's advantage is the rate of fire. Cavour's squint eyes suggested a master manipulator's mind. (See, also, the note on contractions on page 43.)

Use of its/it's. It's means it is, but its denotes possession. *Note: in this instance the apostrophe rule does not apply.* Mistakes with the use of it's/its is widespread in students' work.

The dash (—). Avoid the use of the dash. It can be used instead of the more helpful full stop, colon or semi-colon.

Comments on Style

The three most frequent errors that weaken style are colloquialism, cliché and passive verbs.

Colloquialism is the kind of English you use when talking to your friends. For example, instead of 'Italy, with her beat-up old army, was smashed in North Africa', write 'Italy, her army poorly equipped and without fighting spirit, was soundly defeated in North Africa'.

Clichés are overused words or phrases. Their use lessens the sharpness and strength of your English. You can identify clichés by the frequency with which they are used. Examples include: The Wall Street Crash and depression put the cat among the pigeons for Labour plans in 1931. Germany's defeat at Stalingrad was the moment of truth for Hitler's resistance on the Eastern front.

Passive verbs. The use of passive verbs is the major reason for absence of robust English. Consider this sentence: Grey, returning to office, having seen the support of the people, set about passing the Great Reform Act. Passive verbs are identified by the 'ing' at the end. The sentence expressed with active verbs reads: Grey, who saw the support of the people, returned to office and passed the Great Reform Act.

Dead words and expressions make your English flabby. Dead words include very; totally; quite; extremely; completely; absolutely; really. These words can slip into your essays because we use them when we speak. Some of them, such as completely or totally, weaken what you write by exaggeration. Dead expressions include: It is worthy of note that ... It is not an exaggeration to say that ... It is interesting to note that ...

Tautology is the useless repetition of the same idea in different words. For example: Wilhelm II, troubled and anxious by the Balkan crisis in 1914 … ; The sudden shock of the two nuclear bombs made the Japanese leaders agree to peace.

Avoidance of general adjectives and adverbs. Words such as good, bad, badly, brilliant, dreadful or terrible can be replaced, usually, by more specific words. Example, 'Winston Churchill's party, after doing dreadfully in the 1945 election, became the Opposition.' It would be more effectively expressed as 'Winston Churchill's party lost over half their 387 seats in 1945 and became the Opposition.'

Particular words to use with care or to avoid. These include: just; simply; also; and, especially, get or got. The last two should be replaced by a more specific verb: 'The German army got bogged down at the Marne' should be replaced by 'The German army's advance was halted at the Marne'.

Confusion in the use of effect and affect. Affect means influence. For example, wealthy landowners were affected by the People's Budget in 1909. Effect, which can be used as a verb or a noun, means the reason for some event. For example, Prussia's use of railways effected a rapid victory in 1870. Used as a noun you would write: The effect of the railways was a rapid Prussian victory.

Tone. When you write for your Tutors or Examiners use a tone which is neither deferential nor subservient, as though you cannot know much about the subject; nor patronising, as though the reader does not know as much as you.

Contractions. Do not use contractions (such as, don't, weren't) in essays. Contractions are inappropiate in formal English.

The personal pronoun, I or my. The personal pronoun should not be used in academic answers. If you wish to give particular emphasis that the idea or argument is yours, use the expression 'This writer's view is …'

The Importance of Words

Whereas some academic disciplines, for example Maths, Foreign Languages or Philosophy, require particular aptitudes the foundation requirements for History are an ability to read and write. From this basis the History skills are developed and one of these is language skills. To make a point very strongly, I sometimes tell students that the only equipment needed to make progress in History study are the children's game *Mastermind*, which requires logical thought, and a dictionary. A History-degree course prepares

The Importance of Words

students to be among the thinkers in any branch of life and a thinker has to be able to deal with complicated ideas, enabled by higher-order language skills. Only with a rich vocabulary is it possible to think with the precision needed for complicated ideas and then to communicate them. In an essay *every* word matters, and the use of exactly the right word enhances the quality of your work.

Progress with expression is achieved by awareness of the importance of words and the creation of a rich vocabulary. You may be good at this anyway and widen your vocabulary without difficulty, but if you are not you will benefit from more formal methods. One way is to have a little notebook and jot down words whose meanings you do not know as you read. Then, every week or so, look up the meanings of the new entries in a dictionary and write them in. Words new to you are best remembered by using them, but there are not always occasions to do so and the vocabulary notebook method enables you to skim over entries, now and again, and refresh your memory. In this way you will have more words at your fingertips and you will have taken steps toward being a powerful thinker and communicator.

Spelling. Persistently mis-spelt words weaken a reader's confidence in the writer. Take the trouble to note the correct spelling and add the words with which you have difficulty to the back of your vocabulary book. Words (correctly spelt) which tend to be mis-spelt include: definite, separate, independence, existence, dependant (noun), representative, publicly, benefited, aggressive.

A note on hypocrisy. A hypocrite is a person who does not do what he/she says should be done. Alert readers will conclude that I, the writer of the guide, have not put into practice what I advise. My answer has two parts. First, I purposely did not follow all the advice and introduced a colloquial tone so that the book will seem more approachable to its readers. Second, this is merely a student guide to effective study and not a scholarly student essay.

Key points
- Good English and expression are required for high-grade work.
- Improvement will follow from awareness and attention to detail.
- A rich vocabulary enables effective communication.
- Work for the mastery of English and the refinement of style is a life-long task.

9 Dealing with Deadlines

DEADLINES FOR WORK to be handed to tutors haunt the undergraduate years. Compared to advanced school work there is a greatly reduced programme of obligatory tutorial or lecture attendance and a pleasing absence of nagging teachers. With a huge degree of control over how the days are spent, students' sense of flexibility and freedom is, nevertheless, readily ruined by deadlines. Time can be spent worrying about the deadline and as the date approaches the anxious concern increases. There is, however, a way to deal with this situation: it is to break a task into stages and complete them at a steady pace. This will not mean the abandonment of the freedom for spontaneity in student life.

Setting Your Programmes of Study

You should aim to take control of the deadlines for written work by assigning a programme for each deadline. You may prefer to make this programme in your head, or scribbled on a scrap of paper, or yet more formally in a diary. The programme for any assignment starts from the day the study task is set and runs to the date it is to be presented to your tutor. Students will usually have two or three, maybe as many as five, assignments running in any week. First, for an assignment, write into the programme the completion date of the task at least 24 hours before the tutor's deadline. Thereby you build in a cushion for unforeseen eventualities (a snap decision to go Pennine caving for two days, a visit to Paris ...). The trick is to take control, to do work in *short segments* so that you can see your progress and you are not overawed by a huge task, and to make progress early in the time allowed. Straight away, start the acquisition of books and undertake preliminary reading. It is best to find information early before the last minute panic-driven struggle to find books and sources (see Chapter 2 'Hunting for Information') and your early reading, that is your overview reading, will allow you to absorb the key features of the topic without the pressure of last minute scrambled study. If the work assignment is an essay

Setting Your Programmes of Study **45**

answer, after you have finished your overview reading, prime your mind early by thinking about what could go into the answer. With the question in your mind it will work away on its own so that when you come to prepare the answer (see Chapter 7) you will have more ideas. These preliminaries finished, plan later stages of work and pace them over the available time.

Reasons for Student Underachievement

A programme for work for any study assignment will help to protect you from three reasons for underachievement:

1. Students who work for too long, because they are compulsive bookworms and mistake quantity of study for quality of study.
2. Students who are lazy and study for an insufficient minimum.
3. Students who study ineffectively, however long they study, because they pay little attention to skills and the staging of work.

A programme for a work assignment will help you to move from one level of reading (see Chapter 2) to the next and it will help you to build in the most important and neglected stage of work, working on information (see Chapter 3).

Realistic Daily Objectives and Escape from the Burdens of Study

With, say, four study assignments in progress during any particular week, there may be two or three tasks for you on any working day. They become your (only) two to three tasks for the day - other than obligatory lectures, sports or planned social activity. The tasks should be limited and realistic. When the two or three tasks, which you set at the start of the day, are completed the remaining day (and night) is free. With set tasks, you can have a list in writing or a list in your head, you realistically predefine your day's work. They are more manageable because they are *predefined* and *limited*.

The span of time in which students work well varies. It is best to set yourself a limit and do not be too ambitious to begin with. It is better to work quickly for a short time than to plod on slowly for hours. Even if the span of working time for you is short, with practice it will become longer. However long you work, do not forget to have a break before your next task. Then, by the satisfaction of completed study tasks, you free yourself from the burden of deadlines and free yourself for full participation in non-work student activities. In contrast, the sad student follows undefined, open-ended, study objectives: these are death to substantial progress and a good student life.

Key points
- Take control and make a study programme for each assignment.
- Break the study task into small segments which correspond to the study structure in this guide.
- Set realistic tasks for your programme assignments for each day and when completed end your study.

10 Major Dissertations

WHEREAS COURSE ASSIGNMENTS will be around 2,000 words in length, most courses include options which enable more in-depth work over a longer period and a more substantial dissertation or study which could run from 8,000 to 12,000 words. This work is usually part of the later phase of your course. Chapter 9 is relevant, also, to this bigger assignment and if you have not looked at that chapter I suggest you do so before you read on.

The greater length of time allotted and the more open-ended nature of your dissertation work can lead to even more deadline-related problems. The key to avoid them is to identify the separate study tasks and break your work into separate steps, which you pace yourself to complete, over the whole length of time available.

Subject Choice and Information

In some cases you will be given the topic you are to study: in others you will be left to choose your theme and title. Where you have a choice there are a number of issues to consider.

Bigger assignments, in which you have more freedom to explore your subject and which are less closely supervised by your Tutor, will require more commitment from you. It is important, therefore, to choose a subject which will interest you and sustain your motivation. There is no sense, however, in opting for a topic for which you cannot obtain information and before you settle the subject it is good sense to explore what information you can obtain either immediately or, by ordering from outside libraries, within a short time span. However brilliant or inspiring your projected title is, without accessible information about it you will be unable to write a good assignment. How relevant information can be identified and considered was mentioned in Chapter 2, 'Hunting for Information'.

Break-up of the Dissertation Assignment into Small Steps

With the title settled, your first job is to begin to obtain the information, books, journals, articles and, maybe, videos. Then, unless you are already very familiar with the topic, read a concise account in order to gain an overview. You are now in a position to divide your study into five to nine or so sections. Then loosely divide the time allowed for the assignment into the same number as the sections and focus on one section at a time. Such a division will enable you to pace yourself over the longer than normal time allowedand you have broken the major project into smaller, manageable, parts. As you complete each part you have the satisfaction of your evidential progress to sustain your effort. The greatest reason for under-performance is that students allow time to pass without progress, so the work is crushed into hectic and hasty activity before the deadline.

Investigation-led Study

The surest way to produce a study of substance is to make your work question led. With a fair grasp of the topic after earlier reading, you are in a position to ask demanding questions about the subject: why events happened, why 'x' was important, why the consequences were as they were, and so on. Question-led study will lead you away from a narrative dissertation. Much of your reading will be guided by your search for answers to the questions you generate as you deepen your insights and understanding. Better students will be active, adventurous and resourceful in the search for information.

Tackling Each Step, One at a Time

The questions to which you will seek answers provide the small units, the steps in the bigger study task, and the units of paced work, as you build up your rough draft.

The answers to your questions will be the backbone of your study. Needless to say, you do not write your dissertation in a question and answer form but the content of what you write will be generated by answers to questions. As you read for each part of your study, attention to analysis (Chapter 6) and working on information (Chapter 3) will guide your work away from being only derivative of others. When you read to find answers to your questions, only brief notes are needed before you write your conclusions. In this way, the amount of general note making is reduced and your question answers, one by one, are added together to achieve continuity: they become the first draft of your study.

Tackling Each Step, One at a Time   **49**

Changing a Rough Draft to a Final Draft

Keeping pace with your informal schedule for completion of sections, add to your rough draft, part by part, until your study is finished in rough. When you write your rough draft, it is a good idea to write on every other line: this makes the refinement of your account for the final draft easier. As you work, aim to be prepared to discover new issues which could be considered and to search for new sources. You may find your earlier ideas of the shape of the study change as you progress but this is the sign of your full involvement in the subject.

When you allocate time for your study remember to leave seven to 14 working days to revise and refine your first draft and to write your finished study. You will be surprised by how much you are able to improve your work and improve its shape and tone when you write the finished draft. Only when your study is completed should you write the introduction. Guidance on the format the finished work and the requirements for references to sources and authors will be given by your tutor.

Key points
- Divide your study into sections.
- Have your dissertation under way quickly by starting your first tasks straight away.
- Avoid a passive approach to the subject by a question-led approach.
- Allow several days for the rewriting of your rough draft.

11 Examination Preparation

ALTHOUGH THERE IS VARIATION in university examination arrangements, and coursework contributes to the degree class in many colleges and universities, courses have final exams. My comments apply to preparation for end-of-year examinations as well as to your finals.

Students are Seldom Surprised by Their Degree Class

Very few students are surprised by their degree class when it is published because they have received feedback and comment from their tutors throughout their three years of work. The degree is a reflection of your skills, incrementally developed, your work on the content of your course and your understanding which you developed, month by month, over the course. What is particular about the end of year and, particularly, the final exam is the concentration of assessment, over a few days, of a large part of the course, in timed conditions. This requires the student to have more memorised information and to write a number of answers at speed. There are particular procedures to prepare for this.

There need be nothing daunting about finals. The best way to think about them is to see them as an opportunity - in which you can demonstrate the skills you have developed and your interest in, and understanding of, the past. You cannot deny they are a test, and with your end of course exams, a test with a degree of finality, but all work can be seen as a test. Finals are only a test like any other assignment or like the end of year exams. The difference is the size of the test, but a programme of preparation will enable you to make light of this characteristic.

Your Revision Schedule

The sign of the more adult-minded student is the ability to see not just weeks but months ahead. To pace yourself in preparation for finals you should start to think about them as early as the spring term, weeks before your spring vacation. Find out the date of your first exam (whatever the subject for those who study more than one discipline, as in History and Politics or History and Sociology) and write the date of your first exam in your diary. Then, seven days before, write in the date for completion of all your consolidation work and exam preparation. You may not manage to keep to it exactly but a slightly ambitious date is better than an under-ambitious date. The aim is complete preparation before you sit your first paper. Earlier, measured preparation will release you from last-minute panic and, thereby, increase your confidence. It may, also, give you later some sense of smugness (students are human and open to such feelings) as you observe the manic and inadequate scrablings of the less prepared to botch together revision.

Revision Topic Selection

Having identified your date for the completion of exam preparation you need to identify the topics which you wish to prepare. You may, already, know these from your tutors but even so it is helpful to find whether there are past exam papers. They will probably be in the department library or resource centre and you may be able to buy papers for the past three to four years. It is a good use of resources to pay for photocopies if they can be purchased. Take care to note if the regulations and paper structure will change for your year.

With the information from these past papers and with the help of your tutors, decide on the topics you will prepare for the exams. Don't forget that you will need as many topics to which you are required to write answers plus a few more to give you a choice of questions. If you find you are short of one or two topics you have sufficient time between the spring and the exam to add a topic or two to your portfolio.

When you have chosen your topics you are in a position to allocate time for their revision. Even allowing for a week or two of (complete) holiday at Easter you should have two or so weeks for each topic. Revision can begin as early as February while you continue your course: you do not need to have completed the whole course before you begin. There will be some members of your group, if they hear you have begun revision, who will tell you that you have begun too early but the adult-minded student will ride these comments and nearer the exams you, and not they, will have confidence.

Your Exam Preparation Programme

To an extent your work with preparation will depend on the work you have already undertaken. If you completed any of the suggested activities in the 'Working on Information' in Chapter 3 those notes will be helpful too. The central skills which the exam will assess include:

1. Skills to understand a question and prepare an answer.
2. Skills to express your answer.
3. Your knowledge and understanding of the information and ideas of your topics.
4. Your ability to remember this knowledge.

You will have developed skills 1 and 2 throughout your course (see Chapters 7 and 8). Exam preparation involves transferring No. 3 to No. 4, that is, to your long-term memory.

Revision and Learning Procedure

This is a good way to transfer information to your long-term memory. Assemble all your notes and essays on a topic and from this information create summary sheets - that is pages of information and ideas which condense your earlier notes. There are three great benefits of summary sheets. First, they are a short form of your full notes and, because they are short, they can be scanned quickly in order to refresh your memory. Second, if you follow a similar structure to your earlier notes, when you need to see the longer, more fully explained, notes you will be able to locate details speedily. Third, and most important, the creation of summary sheets lead you to be *active* - to pass the information about the topic through your mind. This activity, itself, will help refresh your memory. Needless to say, the summary sheets should be thoughtfully and attractively laid out - a feature mentioned in Chapter 1 on note making. Once created, much information can be retained by reading your summary sheets several times. Degree-course work requires a substantial foundation of detailed information from which you create your answers and if there are many details which you fail to retain in your memory, consider these procedures drawn from specialists in the psychology of learning.

Increasing the Quantity of Memorised Information

If you consider you are light on factual information you could create a chronology of events, with the help of chronologies published in texts, to add more factual substance to your notes and ideas. If your aim is to learn, for example, a list of 30 dates select just five key dates - one from near the beginning and one from near the end and three others. Learn these by constant repetition. Test your learning by writing out the five dates. Once learned, these five dates will be the 'pegs' to which the other 25 dates will be attached. For each of the five learned dates, remember the dates immediately before and after. Much learning in History uses a process called association. The unremembered (unknown) is remembered by its association with the known. Thereby your first five will become 15 and once you have learned 15, the next 15 can be learned as the gaps between the learned dates. History students are helped because dates may fit into a pattern.

Another method which some students find helpful is to make a recording of notes and to listen to them during other activities, such as journeys.

Short- and Long-term Memory

To convert learned information from short-term memory a phased learning programme will be most effective. The first occasion of learning will be the most demanding and will take longest. When complete, repeat the learning three days later and repeat a third time about eight days later again. Each subsequent session will take less time but remember, reading information without testing, by writing or talking, will reduce the benefit of the time you spend.

Consolidation and learning work is one the more demanding study tasks. It is best not to undertake this in sessions which are too long, until you develop your intellectual stamina and about 60 minutes is more than enough in the earlier weeks. And, because this is less easy work, it is best to undertake it earlier in the day.

Use of a Learned Topic

Once a topic is consolidated use it by applying your knowledge to questions. These you may have gained from past papers (see page 52). All that is required is notes for a skeleton type answer in which you consider the exact question and produce an argument in note form, an argument which will include an overall judgement and the main parts of supporting points with key evidence, arranged in paragraphs (see pages 33-6). These skeleton answers, together with your course work answers, provide prefabricated judgements which you can *apply* to the questions on the paper in the exam room, always taking care to answer the exact question, of course. If you follow these procedures there will be few surprises on the question paper and much of your thinking will have been done during the course and your consolidation and learning. You will be free, thereby, to concentrate on finely crafted and effectively articulated answers.

The Last Twenty-four Hours

Students who phase and pace their revision over the weeks before an exam have an advantage. While others panic and are over anxious well-prepared students are composed and calm during the days before exams begin. How should the last day be spent? With revision finished there are no substantial tasks left but with the nearness of exams inactivity feels out of place. A good way to use the last day is to unstrenuously look over revision notes and, especially, skeleton answers (with their judgements and supporting evidence), thereby to remain active while avoiding the harder work of learning. The night before an exam a glass of beer, or alternative, is in order but do ensure you have a clear head for the exam day!

In the Exam Room

Well-prepared students are composed and calm. This is especially beneficial once you are in the exam room and the awful time arrives to open the question paper. This is the time a few students in every exam make far-reaching errors: it is the time to take the very greatest care.

First, check the instructions just in case the regulations have changed. How many questions must be answered? Is it obligatory to answer questions from particular sections? Once you have confirmed the regulations, read all the questions which relate to the topics you revised and mark every question for which you could write an answer. Then, with the required number of questions in mind, say four, mark and number five questions in order of the highest mark you think you can gain. This is high-speed, intense work because to assess which questions you can answer, you need to run through how you would answer each of them and what information content you would include. In other words, you answer the question rapidly in your mind.

If you are asked to answer four questions why mark your preferences one to five? My reply is that you may find, once you begin an answer, that the question you choose is more difficult than you expected. Your fifth choice is your reserve question and, because it is already chosen, you do not need to spend time and effort on reselecting a question. With the selection completed, begin your first answer. This should be the answer for which you expect the highest mark. Why attempt that question first? Your first answer is the occasion when you introduce yourself to the examiner. A good impression may linger, in second and later answers, longer than is deservesd. You will, also, feel more comfortable and confident with a good answer finished.

One of the great mistakes in exams is to fail to spend an equal length of time on each answer (where each answer carries the same marks): higher marks for an answer on which you spend an unequal time is never sufficient to compensate for loss of marks for a short answer.

Key points
- Start exam preparation early and pace yourself.
- Write summary sheets.
- Develop your long-term memory.
- Ensure you have a full complement of learned information with which you can demonstrate your essays skills.
- Apply learned information to past questions.
- Adapt prepared judgements and collected supporting evidence to answer exam questions.

12 History Writing

Y OU MAY HAVE HEARD the joke about a special type of school pupil who can sit in a class and take information through the ears to the hand which holds a pen, writing notes, without it passing through the brain. Undergraduates are very unlikely to be like that type of pupil and if you have made only some progress with the skills described in this book you will not be one of them. This joke, however, points, at a much more sophisticated level, to the relationship between undergraduate History students and the books they read.

History books which did not carry some reflection of the writer would be as dry as *Kessings Archives,* a weekly publication of news data. A history book is one person's account of the past and in several ways it will reflect the writer. There is a hint of this idea in Hans Holborn's comment 'Knowledge of the past can only be obtained through the subjective experience of the scholar'.

Writers of History and Their Books

A book will reflect the writer in several ways. This can be in the author's chosen focus, say, political history, or economic and social history, cultural history or gender issues. The book will also reflect a style of presentation, say strongly narrative style or a heavily analytical style and the book may be associated with one of the speculative philosophies of history (see Chapter 15). Outside mainline history, the most influential philosophy is Marxism and Christopher Hill's 69-page pamphlet (still in print) *The English Revolution 1640* (1940) is a particularly sharp example of the Marxist interpretation. Beyond these individualities, the writer may favour one form of explanation over another (see Chapter 16). The reality of historical research, in which much evidence on what we really want to know about the past is ambiguous or absent, provides the space to reflect, to some extent, the *writer's* ideas about human beings, the possibilities of human behaviour and the nature of the world.

Critical Readers

As soon as the uncontentious, shorter overview texts are left behind, good readers are alert to notice claims unsupported by convincing evidence, dubious deductions and poor balance in books. Sophisticated students are not passive recipients of a book's contents but intellectually active and critical. They not only read the text but 'read' the standpoint, and the implied assumptions, of the writer. Readers of History should be particularly alert to the choice and use of concepts and terms. They are used by historians, in a way which is not dissimilar to Immanuel Kant's categories (which, he claimed, are the concepts which order our thoughts), *Critique of Pure Reason* (1781), to give coherence to their account of the past and, thereby, they mold their account. Also, a historian's chosen concepts may not be appropiate or valid. If you approach History books in this more critical and 'knowing' way you will gain far more from what you read.

The next section, Thinking About History, is an introduction to the theory of History and historians' exploration of the past.

Critical Readers

Thinking About History

When I was a medical student some pranksters at an end-of-term dance released into the hall a piglet which had been smeared with grease. It squirmed between legs, evaded capture, squealed a lot. People fell over trying to grasp it, and were made to look ridiculous in the process. The past often seems to behave like that piglet.

Julian Barnes, *Flaubert's Parrot.*

13 The Student and Theory

Y OU MAY ASK why this part of the book is added to a study
guide. After all, you have studied History for several years with
sufficient success to be accepted for degree course study and you
have not needed theory, so why consider the theory of History now?

Consider this make-believe example. If you were asked to
volunteer to make up numbers in an American football team but
you had never played before, or even seen a game, and did not
know the aims or procedures, you would not be an effective team
member. Your movements in the game could well resemble those of
a headless chicken. When you know the aims of the game, the rules,
and the patterns and procedures of play, you will read the game
better, both as a participant and as an observer, and be in the
position to contribute to your team's success and to your enjoyment.

Reasons for Thinking about History

So far, in your successful study of History, you have mostly used
heavily synthesised accounts in textbooks or short student introduc-
tions, but as a degree-course student you are closer to the research
historian and over your years of study you will have the
opportunity to use the writing of research historians: writing which
is different from textbooks. An awareness of the historical enterprise
will help you to use degree-course texts and research historians'
work in academic journals or essay collection more effectively.

There are four further reasons why you should consider the
theory of History. First, you will agree, that the content of History
you studied, and your appreciation of History, have changed from
when you were 9, or 15, or 17-years-old. Primary school History,
with romance and heroism and great simplification was very
different from advanced History with its detail, analysis, and
political, social and economic focuses. Some understanding of the
theory of History is a further development towards an even more
sophisticated view of History. Second, as an undergraduate closer to
research historians, an awareness of the historical enterprise, its aims

Reasons for Thinking about History **61**

and procedures, and the difficulties of the historical discipline, will raise your understanding and appreciation of what you read. Third, many undergraduate courses have a theory or historiography component or module and you may find these few pages serve as an introduction to that part of your course. And, fourth, you are now more advanced members of an academic discipline but even at this stage, there is still little scope for you to add to the knowledge of History instead of reading and considering what others have added. An awareness of the theory of History, however, will give you an added perspective, encourage you to a deeper reflection on what you read and make you a more effective History student.

Students Do Not Always Find the Theory of History Easy

You will probably find these pages, especially Chapter 16, less easy than the rest of this book. If you become bogged down with Chapter 16, Key Critical Questions, it is suggested you go on to the next chapter and return to it at a later time when you are more ready to tackle those themes.

The following pages are a snapshot overview of the topic. Once you have gained a further appreciation of the historical enterprise, these pages will have served their purpose. If you are engaged by the issues in this short introduction to the theory of History, you will find suggestions for further reading at the end of the book.

14 The History of History

I T SEEMS there have been stories about the past as long as human societies existed and at some stage these stories, remembered and passed from generation to generation, were written down. Some chapters of the Bible's Old Testament, such as Exodus, Joshua, Judges and Kings, are examples. A wish for a sense of the past is inseparable from our humaneness. Herodotus and Thucydides, both Greeks, in the fifth century BC wrote of wars as did the Roman writers Livy (59 BC - AD 17), Tacitus (AD 55-120) and Plutarch (AD 50-120). The form was a story of political and military events and from these histories, it was assumed, lessons could be learned.

Medieval Histories and Early-Modern Historians

After the collapse of the Roman Empire, events of History were recorded by the ecclesiastical chroniclers, of whom Bede (672/3-735) is a well-known example. These chronicles included little reflection or comment and an uncritical acceptance of sources. Medieval historians, such as Froissart (c. 1337-c. 1410), were influenced by St Augustine (see page 67) and although they, too, tended to be uncritical of sources, they had some idea of historical perspective but were inclined to see events as the judgement of God. It was not until the Renaissance period, with its broader appreciation of mankind and a more critical approach to sources, that changes in writing about the past were accomplished. Although both Machiavelli, noted for his handbook on political action, *The Prince*, and Guicciardini, wrote about recent history, the Italian Wars, they took as their focus the evidence and what arguments could be drawn from it. In England James I's former Lord Chancellor, Sir Francis Bacon, in *The History of Henry VII* (1622), wrote from a detailed examination of the evidence from which he sought to draw out the reasons for events.

The religious strife in the sixteenth and seventeenth centuries and the destruction and dispersal of records, which are the historians' foundation material, was the background to much

Figure 15. Leopold von Ranke (left) and Fernand Braudel (see page 66)

activity in locating and recollecting documents, both religious and secular, and the compilation of texts such as those of the Jesuits' *Acta Sanctorum*, and to a greater awareness of their value.

Leopold von Ranke

Widely accepted as the first historian in the sense the word is used today, because he founded his work on the stringently critical use of a wide range of sources, Leopold von Ranke (1795-1886), published his first book *The Roman and German Peoples* in 1824. He was appointed professor of History in Berlin in 1835 and it was his use of extensive records which included diaries, letters, diplomatic and state papers, from many archives (he visited Germany, Austria, France, Italy and England), and his seminars in Berlin on research techniques, which contributed to further developments in historical study. An École des Chartes, to train students in the use of historical sources, was founded in Paris in 1821, and a chair of History in the Collège de France was established in 1831. Much impetus was given to the work with the creation of substantial collections, such as *Monumenta Germania Historia*. The Historical Manuscripts Commission was established in Britain rather later under the influence of William Stubbs, the Regius Professor at Oxford, in 1870.

Narrative History

Macaulay (1800-1859) is the modern historian most associated with narrative History. Trained as a lawyer, Macaulay was for most of his life a politician but in 1850 he retired in order to write his *History of England*, five volumes of which were published. While his *History* is criticised for viewing England's past from the standpoint of the mid-nineteenth-century parliamentary constitution, he portrayed the past as an enthralling drama through which he masterfully wove strands of several themes. Later British examples of this genre include J.E. Neale's *Queen Elizabeth I* and, in recent times, Simon Schama's *Citizens*.

The Widening Focus

Ranke's *History* centred on politics and the development of the state but the narrow focus was questioned by later historians and by a greater recognition of the work of earlier writers, such as Robertson in Scotland (1735-1801), who had given weight to social as well as political History and Johann von Herder (1744-1803) had written on the influence of geography in history and history's onward march. Herder had, also, acknowledged a duty to understand the past in the context of that time. Jacob Burckhardt (1818-1897), wrote not on the state but on culture and the civilisation of Renaissance Italy.

Economic History

Henri Pirenne (1862-1935) grounded his work on the sources after the manner of Ranke. While studying Belgian towns and cities he was drawn to economic dimensions of life, most notably illustrated by his *Medieval Cities* published in 1922. Economic History became an interest in Britain, as illustrated by R.H. Tawney (1880-1962), whose *The Agrarian Problem in the Sixteenth Century*, was published in 1912, and in particular by J.H. Clapham (1873-1946). Initially professor in Leeds, John Clapham gained access to industrial records and his first book, *The Woollen and Worsted Industries*, was published in 1907. He is, however, best remembered for a huge work, published in three volumes between 1926 and 1938, *An Economic History of Modern Britain*, by which time most university departments had economic History specialists.

Annales Historians

In this century the further widening of the historian's field of study has been led most notably by the French *Annales* historians, named after the journal of that name founded in 1929 by Lucien Febve (1878-1956) and Marc Bloch (1886-1944). The editors aimed to encourage 'total' History which would encompass economic, social, cultural and intellectual History while retaining rigorous standards of scholarship. This ambitiously wide spectrum of study required competence in more skills than mere critical documentary research. Bloch, for example, studied archaeology, agronomy, cartography, folk-lore and linguistics. It is from within the *Annales* tradition that Fernand Braudel (1902-1985) wrote arguably the most influential work of the twentieth century, *The Mediterranean and The Mediterranean World in the Age of Philip II* (1949).

This brief survey of the History of History is intended to identify its main marker posts. Excluded from this chapter are writers who worked within the field of History and contributed to the philosophy of History and they are considered in the next chapter.

15 The Philosophy of History

THE WORD PHILOSOPHY is given different meanings, dependent upon the context of its use. Karl Popper claimed that we are all philosophers in the sense that we all have a body of working principles and beliefs, more or less consistently and coherently held together, by which we live our lives. Here the word is used to refer to the exploration of the general principles of History and its study. What this meaning implies is a consideration of the assumptions that lie behind the study of History and/or that underlie history. In this sense the philosophy of History falls into two parts: the critical philosophy of History (the theme of the next chapter) and the speculative philosophy of History, which is the content of this chapter. Those who have contributed to the speculative philosophy of History, who look below the surface of events and changes, have sought to identify the purpose, or meaning, or the underlying pattern, of history.

St Augustine and the *City of God*

Augustine, a convert to Christianity, Bishop of Hippo (North Africa) from 396, completed the 22 books of *The City of God* by 426. Writing within the contemporary tradition, in which the work of God was seen in history, Augustine wrote about Rome, its History and fall and the reasons for Rome's defeat. From that beginning he traced the History of religious thought, pagan and Christian, the creation of the world and the place of Christ in history and, latterly, the nature of man and the purpose of life. What distinguishes his work, and makes it worthy of consideration today, is the book's reflection of the scholarship and intellectual power of Augustine and the coherence and thoroughness of his account.

Kant, Herder, Hegel

Immanuel Kant (1724-1804), best known for his massive contribution to epistemology (the theory of knowledge), approached history from the direction of moral philosophy and he made no pretence to be well informed of the details of History. He saw history made sense as a progression toward a better state of affairs. This progression is not evident if individual lives are considered, at which level history seems incoherent and chaotic, but a deeper purpose may be seen if the History of Man is viewed over centuries. This purpose is the consequence of the nature of Man and Man's potentialities. Mankind wishes to act only for selfish needs, answerable only to the individual's will, but this leads to separateness from others: on the other hand Man needs to live with others in order to express and develop inherent capacities. This wish for self fulfilment leads Man to develop the arts of life in society. Further, societies and states, because of conflicts between them, are drawn towards cohabiting in a confederation of nations and to an acceptance of an authority over all its members.

Herder's philosophy of history is found in his *Ideas for a Philosophical History of Mankind* (1781), a huge work in which he outlines astronomy, geomorphology, plant and animal life and the special characteristics of the human species, as well as the influence of geography and climate on history. Herder saw history as the interplay of two kinds of forces: the external forces, represented by society, and internal forces, the spirit of the people in which societies are gathered. Herder's philosophy emphasised, first, that events should not be seen as lawless but the result of circumstances in which they took place, including the internal forces. In that way Herder viewed History as he viewed natural science. Second, he claimed, history should be seen to have a purpose, and that purpose was to be found within Man's potentialities, the attainment of humanity, which would be achieved when Man becomes truly human.

Hegel (1770-1831) became professor of History in Berlin in 1818 and his philosophy of history was summarised in *Lectures on the Philosophy of History*, published posthumously in 1837. In these lectures he described the pattern of history, which he saw as a manifestation of spirit which developed by an inner logic, the dialectic progression. In this, opposing demands (thesis and antithesis) are resolved by a compromise (synthesis). Below the confusion of events, and central to history, was the idea of freedom and its increasing embodiment in institutions. In ancient societies only one, the despot, was free; in Greece and Rome some, the citizens, were free: but in the constitutional monarchies of Hegel's day there was the institutional possibility of all being free.

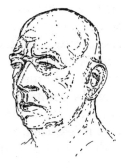

Figure 16. Karl Marx and Oswald Spengler (see page 70)

Karl Marx

Since the latter years of the nineteenth century the ideas of Karl Heinrich Marx (1818-1883) have had an immense influence on historical scholarship and his ideas command attention even after the collapse of the USSR, whose founders were profoundly influenced by Marx. Based on his interest in industrial History and politics, which he shared with his friend and collaborator Friedrich Engels, Marx developed a theory of History which was most fully worked out in *German Ideology* but which is in outline in *Manifesto of the Communist Party*, first published in 1848. No student can fail to be stimulated by this short work which runs to only 16 sides of A4.

Fundamental to Marx's thought is his notion of dialectical materialism. By materialism Marx claimed that the means of production (economics) was the dominant influence in History, including its politics, society and culture, and the idea of the dialectic which Marx took from Hegel (page 68). There are, within any society, claimed Marx, both economic structures and political structures. The economic structures, the means of production, had been, in broad terms, the nomadic, the feudal and, latterly, the capitalist. Marx's particular claim was that economic change provided the dynamic of history because the owners of the means of production gain command of the state and control of its laws and government. As the feudal means of production gives way to the capitalist (Marx wrote when some states were capitalist, others were not) and new owners of the means of production emerge, so the old class, the word used by Marx to describe those with a common relationship to the means of production, who had control of the state, would be displaced by the new class, the capitalist owners of the new means of production.

From this starting point, Marx predicted the future.

Karl Marx   **69**

Competition was at the centre of the capitalist means of production, said Marx. Competition would both drive the less successful businesses into bankruptcy but those who did not fail would have to reduce wages and harshen working conditions to succeed in the competitive environment. It was in this situation, said Marx, that the workers, in desperation, would revolt, take control of the state and reform the organisation of production and the ownership of property. It is less clear from Marx's writings where Mankind would progress after 'the revolution', through the dialectic, thereafter.

Spengler and Toynbee

Spengler (1880-1936), formerly a schoolmaster, published the two volumes of his *The Decline of the West* in 1918 and 1922 and immediately gained wide notoriety. Spengler saw the history of the world as eight discreet cultures which included the Egyptians, Indians and, more latterly, the Appollinian (Greece and Rome), Magian (mostly Islam) and the culture of the West - this latter culture spanned the last millennium. Cultures had a necessary pattern of growth, maturity and decay and each had a unique orientation which is expressed in all aspects of life, political, economic or cultural. Influenced by Nietzsche, Spengler claimed a culture declined to become mere civilisation in its phase of decay. In the case of the West, this stage would be characterised by the all-consuming world city, materialism, tyranny and warfare, and this, wrote Spengler, had begun. Spengler's *Decline* may entertain through its boldness and dogmatism but gains little respect as a contribution to philosophy of history.

Toynbee (1889-1975), appointed director of studies at the Royal Institute of International Affairs in London in 1924, was interested in the seeming repetition of patterns in history and, later, in the origins of civilisation. It was in this context that he read Spengler's *Decline of the West* and although there is some superficial similarity, both men describe the rise, flowering and decline of civilisations, their work moved in different directions. Toynbee published 12 volumes of *A Study of History* between 1934-61 in which he describes the rise and decline of 21 civilisations. His over-arching analysis was the place of challenge, and response to challenge, as the reason for the robustness or decline of a civilisation. Toynbee's books, huge in scale, achieved wide prominence but he was more admired by the History reading public than by fellow historians, who criticised him for contorting information to fit his alleged patterns of history.

16 Key Critical Questions

C ONTRIBUTORS TO THE SPECULATIVE philosophy of history may have excited readers by the broad sweep of history they cover, by the boldness of assertion or by the penetrative insights they present but few who consider them find them fully satisfactory. Over the last 100 or so years grand theory, such as speculative philosophies of history, has received less attention than the critical philosophy of History and it is to the questions asked most frequently in this area of study to which I turn now.

Is History a Science?

In medieval time 'science' referred to any branch of knowledge and what is popularly now called Science was distinguished from other areas of study by the name 'natural philosophy'. It is now held by many that among the branches of knowledge, Science, its content and the methods by which it is studied, has the highest esteem. In so far as another branch of knowledge, such as Psychology or History, is to a greater extent scientific so it, too, is received with more confidence and higher esteem.

Science receives so much respect because of the usefulness of Science for the improvement of the standard of life through technology. There are, however, misconceptions about Science: the *essence* of science is not *to explain* but *to describe* what is the case. This is not to say that, in everyday speech, we do not talk of scientific explanation. What is meant by explanation is a complete description of the influences on a phenomenon and all the reasons for a change in its state. A full description is possible because in everyday Science (exclusive of quantum physics) the 'horizon' of influence (beyond which we do not need to search) is limited and unchanging. The world of, say, physics or chemistry, has no history but a repetitions regularity and one description of a circumstance will be the same as any other description of the same circumstance. Hydrogen and oxygen mixed in a particular proportion will always constitute water and the properties of copper are the same today as it was in

Ancient Greece. It is from this regularity that so-called scientific 'laws' are proposed. These 'laws' are not like the laws of a state's legal system but only the summation of observances which prove to be, time after time, always the same. The central philosophic problem in Science is that it is not in essence deductive (whereby a particular case is taken from the general) but inductive: a general claim, or 'law of science', is asserted from particular instances, and the 'law' is accepted only until observation shows it is inaccurate or incomplete. It must be said that popular Science, Science as understood by people and students up to the end of school, is simpler Newtonian Science. Modern theoretical Science, such as theoretical physics, since the work of Clerk Maxwell (1831-1879) and the recognition of force fields and quantum physics, in which greater weight is given to the probationary status of theories and the more subjective nature of models, whether represented by mathematics or diagrams, to describe the form and forces in physics does not belong within the popular, simpler, idea of science. The probationary nature of Science gained more widespread recognition after the publication of Thomas Kuhn's *The Structure of Scientific Revolutions* (1962) and the popularisation of the notion of paradigm.

With this widely held misconception in mind, the similarities and differences of History and Science are clearer. Both are concerned with observation of the evidence and a description of what is, or in the case of History, what was, the circumstance or event and both are concerned to find the *connection* between one circumstance or event and another. Whereas the scientist, studying the natural world which demonstrates constants and *regularities,* can infer a future connection between circumstances, and propose a 'law' and go on to verify it against further observations, historians who study *particulars* without these regularities can only describe things as they were. History, in addition, has a denser connectiveness than science. John Passmore, in an essay in which he uses seven criteria to compare the work of the scientist and the historian, concludes: 'If we mean by "science" the attempt to find out what really happens, then History is a science. It demands the same kind of dedication, the same ruthlessness, the same passion for exactness, as physics. That is all I have been trying to show. If, however, we mean by science the search for general theories, then History is not science.'

What the historian cannot do, unlike the scientist, is to create an experiment which exactly repeats past circumstances. It has to be added, also, that History, unlike Science, does not enable prediction except of the most general and trite kind. Further, unlike Science, History has an 'inward facet' (see page 74) apart from the outward world of events. It can be concluded that in the methods of study, both holding the primacy of evidence, Science and History are as one. Although History lacks the regularities of simpler, Newtonian, Science the differences between the disciplines of science and History is less great when comparison is made with frontier-research theoretical Science.

What is Explanation in History?

Note. The inappropiateness of the use of 'explanation' has been mentioned (page 71). It is employed here only because its use is so widespread and it is used in the quoted passages. Its substitution here with the more accurate 'description' could confuse readers.

Of all the questions considered in the critical philosophy of History none has attracted so much attention as explanation. Explanation can be taken to mean a full description of the reasons for events. Three kinds of answers have been given to this question.

The Covering Law Theory. Carl Hempl, a philosopher of Science, in his covering law theory, claims History, as a branch of knowledge, is in essence the same as the empirical sciences such as physics or biology and that explanation is achieved, and only achieved, by subsuming what is to be explained under a general law. The laws most relevant are those of the social sciences, such as those of psychology, sociology and economics. However, it must be noted that in these branches of knowledge 'laws' have been established less successfully than in the natural sciences and, anyway, Hempl admits that historians, compared with scientists, explain with a looser 'explanatory sketch'. Michael Stanford in *The Companion to the Study of History,* in a measured discussion of Hempl's theory, gives this example:

> In *The Making of Victorian England,* G. Kitson Clark discusses the rapid growth of population in the first half of the nineteenth century. How is it to be explained? Immediate explanations point to a rise in the birth rate and a fall in the death rate. But why these? The greater availability of medical facilities, increase in medical skills, improvements in hygiene and widespread vaccination are among the reasons put forward for the latter. The former

What is Explanation in History?

can be accounted for by a lowering of the marriage age for women and a higher proportion of marriageable women actually marrying. These, in turn, can be explained by a slackening of customary precautions against early or foolish marriages because fewer employees lived in the households of their masters. This, both in town and country, results from changes in industrial and agricultural techniques. Thus suggested explanations make use of natural (especially biological) laws, and also refer to widespread changes in technology, in the economy, in society and in customs. Here, I think, Hempel's case is made: that historians frequently appeal to empirically established laws or regularities by way of explanation or, at least, they offer explanatory sketches along these lines.

Hempl's form of explanation can contribute to explanations but it is insufficient by itself. Several criticsms can be made. Sometimes historians ask not *why* but *how* something happened or, even, how was it that something did *not* happen, and they seek to explain not only events but actions and ideas - where logical deduction from a law is inapplicable. An even greater objection to this form of explanation is the historian's concern with the unique. Although circumstances, on different occasions, may be similar, because of people's memory of earlier circumstances about which it must be assumed people have an awareness, a historical dimension is added to every event. Further, behind the covering law theory is the idea of necessity (which will be considered later) and predictability: indeed, Hempl claimed an explanation 'is not complete unless it might as well have functioned as a prediction'. Historians, however, ask not 'why must?' type questions so much as 'how possibly?' questions. While covering law reasons often form *part* of explanation for History, because of the central place of Man these reasons are usually insufficient to provide a full explanation.

Rational-purposive explanation. This is an alternative form of explanation. Wilhelm Dilthey (1833-1911), the German philosopher, was an early proposer of this form. For Dilthey, writes Gordon Leff, 'History was about intelligent individuals acting according to purposes and within a defined cultural framework of institutions, traditions, beliefs, laws and values, which characterise different societies and epochs and the individuals who lived in them. History was, therefore, concerned with what he called a mind-affected world, as the work of human agency, whose past, no less than its present, could only be understood by penetrating beyond the outer expressions, or objectifications as he called them, of human activities and values, whether of a society or an individual, to their inner meaning in the experience and intentions of their agents.' Here the idea of the separateness of the outside of history, the events, and the inside, is made. A full understanding of history needs to encompass both. The ascription of meaning to expression through action was possible because of the common humanity of the historian and the people studied. This position is not dissimilar to that of R.G. Collingwood (1889-1943) who wrote in his *An Autobiography* 'You are thinking historically ... when you say about anything, "I see what the person who made this (wrote this, used this, designed this, etc.) was thinking" ... there is nothing else except thought that can be the object of historical knowledge'. But if we accept people can be impelled to act from feelings, fear, hate, ambition and so on, these are not open to rethinking and the way people thought in different cultures will require the historian to inform himself/herself widely before we can fairly share a common culture and study History from 'the inside'.

The narrative form of explanation. This is the third approach and I take Michael Oakeshott, a political philosopher, to represent this form. He summarised his ideas by three essays which were published in *On History* (1983). They are not easy reading in which Oakeshott, in the delivery of a tight and thorough discussion, claims that the object of historians' study is events: periodisation, such as 'the Reformation', 'the industrial revolution', 'the cold war' and so on, are not part of the content of History but terms imposed on it by historians, as also are concepts, such as cause. His central contention can be summarised in his own words.

> What I am seeking is, then, the kind of relationship which, when in an historical enquiry it is found to subsist between antecedent events and a subsequent event, composes an identity which may be described, alternatively, as an event properly understood as an outcome of antecedent events, or as an assemblage of events related in such a manner as itself to constitute an historically understood event. I shall call it a contingent relationship. ...
>
> This kind of relationship is, first, one of proximity and of 'touch'; an immediate relationship. An historical past,

What is Explanation in History? **75**

composed conceptually of contiguous historical events has no place for extrinsic general terms of relationship - the glue of normality or the cement of general causes. When an historian assembles a passage of antecedent events to compose a subsequent he builds what in the countryside is called a 'dry wall': the stones (that is, the subsequent event) are joined and held together, not by mortar, but in terms of their shapes. And the wall, here, has no premeditated design; it is what its components, in touch, constitute.

Oakeshott draws attention to the illegitimacy of all but events and proven connections between events in accounts of the past. This excludes the concepts which historians bring into their writing to order, shape and bind events. Oakeshott, however, writes as a political philosopher and the type of History most suitable for this single-minded approach is the political past.

What is the Place of Causation in History?

The idea of causation plays a part in explanation. Cause is a word used by scientists. Because of the regularities in science, its 'laws', it can be said, for example, that the cause, in terms of chemistry and physics, of the explosion in the garden shed was the schoolboy's (experimental) mix of chemicals commonly called sugar and weedkiller. Ludwig Wittgenstein's *Philosophical Investigations* (1958) alerts us to the way we can be misled by words. The same word can have alternative meanings when used under different 'rules'. A chequer board always has the same squares but, dependent on the rules, it can be used for draughts or for chess. Cause, with its assumption of regularity and necessity, is a word suitable for use with science. The appropriate word for History with looser, less necessary, connections is reason.

When historians present the reasons why an event occurred, they may give different categories of reasons: reasons from nature (global warming, agricultural production, black death ...) or technology (Sadam stunned by cruise missiles ...), and reasons from the regularity of society, its laws and customs (sixteenth-century Spanish land law led to depopulation of the countryside) or Man's wishes, will or intention (Bismarck decided on war against Denmark in 1864).

Historians distinguish between necessary and sufficient reasons. A necessary reason is one without which something cannot happen -

fuel is necessary to make an internal combustion engine work - while a sufficient reason is one where a consequence always follows. Historians tend to look for sets of sufficient reasons. If there are two states with conflicting interests and a refusal to compromise, both strongly armed and capable of war, and both with a strong belief they can win, historians will claim the sufficient reasons for a war are present. When historians assemble a set of sufficient reasons the place of coincidence is significant. The coincidence of a weak government, enfeebled by war, and a revolutionary movement, provide two sets of reasons, which *together*, are sufficient reasons for change while each set alone is not.

What is accepted as a reason by historian or reader can depend upon their interest. R.G. Collingwood provided an example:

> ... a car skids while cornering at a certain point, strikes the kerb and turns turtle. From the car-driver's point of view the cause of the accident was cornering too fast, and the lesson is that one must drive more carefully. From the county surveyor's point of view the cause was a defect in the surface or camber of the road, and the lesson is that greater care must be taken to make roads skid-proof. From the motor-manufacturer's point of view the cause was defective design in the car, and the lesson is that one must place the centre of gravity lower.

Historians do not only search for the reasons for events but also evaluate them and propose one or more have greater importance. By importance they claim either, that the particular reason was the immediate one for an event - take that last reason away and the event could not have happened - or, that it changed what can reasonably be expected might have occurred. Such a calculation is a matter of judgement by the historian, based on information and experience, and uses counterfactuals (see page 21). As Michael Stanford, in *The Companion to the Study of History*, writes:

> ... without deciding what is significant the historian can hardly write at all; he does not know what to put in and what to leave out. Yet all judgements about significance, importance, necessity, causal force and so on involve assumptions about what did not happen - assumptions about what would have happened if ... in short, counter-factual assumptions. Thus counter-factual conditionals are

What is the Place of Causation in History?

quite indispensable for the historian, and yet they must remain mere supposition. They are no more than estimates of probability. ... Without making judgements about the significance of events, without judging the nature of causal forces in history, of necessity and sufficiency, of the relative importance of this or that causal factor, the historian cannot work at all. Such judgements constitute the very essence of history.

Is History Determined? What of Free Will?

Those who accept the methodological correctness of the covering law form of explanation can be expected to say history is determined and that causes can be found if only historians gain sufficient evidence. I have already questioned the usefulness of the use of the scientific term 'cause' by historians: I now go further to say the notion of determinism is unhelpful. This is not to deny that there are always reasons for events and for changes but history has a denser, more complicated, mesh of influences than science, not to mention the place of Man and of intention and will in history. A further complication is historical memory and the absence of science-like 'laws' of human behaviour. It is these which make the idea of determinism inappropriate. It is enough that historians establish what really happened and why it happened by the identification of the reasons.

If it is not useful to say history is determined, does Man have free will? Not necessarily. Philosophers who consider the question generate disagreement when they make wide generalisations. We do, however, live under personal restraints of various kinds. For example, however much I tried I could not become a 100 metre champion, but I could cut down the number of cups of coffee I drink. For a more satisfying assessment of free will a complicated categorisation of areas of action and strong or weak influences on the possibilities of action is required and such analysis would vary from person to person and be dependent on position in a span of time.

Truth and Objectivity

Truth in History is not the same as truth in, for example, Science. In History truth is about the past and a particular part of the past, such as the Peasant's Revolt of 1381 or the Great Reform Act, 1832. Truth in History is a collection of true statements which are founded on evidence. The great majority of evidence in History is not direct evidence, that is not direct experience through our senses, but indirect evidence, such as diaries, memoirs, state papers, maps, which collectively are called documentary evidence, as well as relics, ruins, buildings, artefacts and so on. True statements will be consistent with the evidence. This is easily said but in practice matters are more difficult because evidence does not by itself constitute a historical account, but only information which can contribute to an account. Evidence has to be assessed, interpreted and its meaning established (see next chapter, page 81). In addition, the historian looks to the evidence to find out not only what happened but why it happened.

Truth in History is both a property of statements and a goal. Bit by bit evidence is assembled and scrutinised and the circumstances of the past presented in an account which not only corresponds with the evidence but also achieves coherence. Needless to say, much is absent in any collection of true statements about the past and it is easier to identify false statements than to make swift progress to a complete, and completely true, account.

If this appears to be difficult and uncertain you should remember that those who study the past are not isolated but members of a community of historians, and a historian's work with evidence and an account of the past is subjected to the rigorous scrutiny of others who are well placed to question the correctness, that is the truthfulness, of what is written. In this scrutiny the disinterested objectivity of the historian is checked. It is the openness of the historian's workings which provides a check to bias or prejudice.

It is in this way, in the answerability of historians, and the discourse (and sometimes controversy) among historians, that a greater fullness and certainty in knowledge, and steps toward the truth of the past, is achieved. Michael Stanford has written: 'Historical knowledge does not consist of a set of exactly and unquestionably true statements. Rather it is a web of mutually limiting statements or beliefs, few if any of which are absolutely certain. Yet, taken together they form a consistent and very probable whole. It is like trying to arrive at a point by a number of intersecting loops. Although we sometimes stress the differences among historians, it is surprising how very much they agree.'

17 The Past and History

T HE PAST. The subject of History is Mankind in society in the past, a past that was a present. Unlike the present, in which it is possible to visit and question and re-question people, the actors in history, access to the past is only through remaining evidence. Since Medieval times the most substantial category of evidence is documents. Whereas for Medieval History the number of extant documents is limited, after the eighteenth century the quantities of documentary evidence is huge. After the occupation of Berlin in 1945, for example, lorry upon lorry of documents were removed by the Allies. With such extensive evidence, historians of recent history rely on the help of the record officer and classifier to help the location, assessment and selection of evidence. Since the invention of photography and moving film, visual evidence has become abundant and, in the last few years, the internet has created a new source of evidence.

History's Constituency

History, as knowledge, is part of a seamless panorama of knowledge which ranges from astronomy, physics, geology, politics, sociology, psychology, theology and so on. These segments of knowledge are defined by us by their subject and each has its procedures of study. Each is part of History's constituency in so far that each is open to a study of its history: the History of science, the History of theological, geological, astronomical, or sociological study and even the History of History. The distinctiveness of History as a branch of knowledge is the focus on the past and its method in which surviving evidence of the past is used.

It is the primacy of evidence as the basis for the historian's work which parallels that of the scientist. The importance of evidence is illustrated by the citation of documents in research historian's scholarly papers and monographs, a practice which enables others to follow the research historian's path through the evidence to check the validity of the claims made.

Although, unlike scientists who work within the regularities of nature, historians cannot gain additional evidence by a rerun of an experiment, the repeated interrogation of the evidence by different historians creates the agreement about the past among those who study it.

History and Evidence

History, in the sense of written accounts of the past, is not formed by a direct transposition of evidence in a patchwork quilt, cut and paste manner but from its selection, criticism and interpretation. Historians work in three areas before evidence can be useful.

1. Assessment of the genuineness and reliability of the evidence. This will include information about its origin and the possession of the evidence until the historians use it. Did those who kept the evidence tamper with it? Forgery is not unknown, the purported Hitler Diaries published by *The Times* is a notorious example. When it is accepted that the evidence, say a document, is genuine what of its reliability? Was the writer in a position to know what is claimed - about, for example, where a riot began, or the quantity of armaments stockpiled? Was the writer's intention to be truthful or was the document written to varnish the truth and persuade a reader? Even if the writer wanted to present a truthful picture did prejudice bias or exaggeration distort what was written?

2. The question of language, content and meaning. Documents in the historian's own language, even from a few decades before will embody different idioms and ways of expression which make difficult the educement of subtlety and nuance, which can be so important for understanding the real content of evidence. The difficulties of language are, of course, much greater with documents from more distant times or documents in foreign languages. Further, events before, and the circumstances in which it was written, needs to be known for the historian to obtain a more complete understanding of evidence.

3. Interpretation. When the historian is satisfied with the genuineness of an item of evidence, interpretation is required: that is, the meaning and significance of the evidence must be decided. It is then that the historian can use that evidence in the work of production of an account of the past.

Reforming the Past in the Mind of the Historian

Working from the sources, historians do not only seek to answer

Reforming the Past in the Mind of the Historian

questions on what happened and who was involved but also how and why it happened, and what were the *connections* between events. From the answers to these questions a 'picture' and understanding of the past is formed in the mind of the historian. As historians move forward their enquiries, in particular from what happened, to the reasons why they happened, it is not unlikely that there will be an absence of evidence, however exhaustive the researches. In an attempt to provide a full account of the past, historians call upon generalisations about the possibilities of human nature, and the way the world is, judiciously applied to the particular situations. In short, historical study draws its students to a deeper appreciation of life. This structure can be crudely expressed as an inverted triangle.

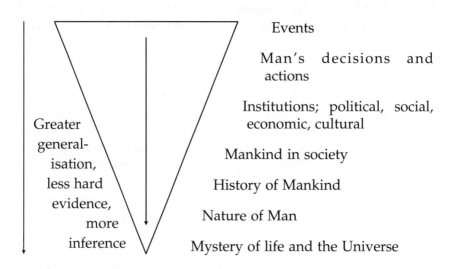

Figure 17. Full accounts of the past call upon generalisation about human nature

Dealing with the absence of hard evidence is more acute in the study of the History of more intangible phenomena such as a society's collective memory (Northern Ireland, or France in 1830 are examples), the History of style or the study of the changes in the spirit of the age (the *Zeitgeist*), topics which some students find stimualting. Such subjects are less served by documentary evidence and finding connections from foundation influences and tracing their transmission and evolution provides many problems - but this kind of study, whatever the difficulties, is enthralling and helps us understand our society, and ourselves, today.

Communicating History

To be communicated to readers the historian's picture of the past is presented in prose which, because of the structure of language, and to help clarity, favours a substantially linear account. From this a line of connections - say a sequence of economic changes during the industrial revolution, or social or political change - is described and explained.

Writers of History can be influenced by the preoccupations of the contemporary world in the choice of subject. To effectively convey a picture of the past they will use the language of the present, including the telling expressions which carry meaning at the time. Language and expression are dynamic: only by using the expressions of the present can the writer of History lead the reader to a surer grasp of the past. For this reason, it can be argued, History should be rewritten for every generation if the truth of the past is to be conveyed.

The constraints of producing a written account of the past impose focus on the writer. Only a great literary and intellectual talent, such as Macaulay, successfully writes an account with many interweaving threads. Often, no more than one main thread is managed in an account, say gender History presented within the political, economic and social context, or cultural History within the social and economic context. Over the last decades there have been historians who have looked at the past from newer perspectives: not from the perspective of high politics, that is government policy and its imposition on 'the people', that is History from above. Instead, 'History from below' has been written, accounts of the lives of those who had no part in politics but whose lives were acted upon by governments. The point is that the perspective is limited. An apple, suspended by a thread from its stalk in front of you cannot be seen except from the direction from which you look at it, but that view of the apple is incomplete. The best you can do is to surround it with mirrors, on its sides and above and below and, although you will have only one view at a time, move your eyes quickly between the mirrors in order to have a complete view. To ask which focus is better is to ask someone whether they prefer oranges or pears: the preference, for research historians, History students or readers of History, is a personal choice. If utility is considered, an industrialist is more likely to gain more benefit by reading economic History, especially an account of his/her industry, than cultural History. To gain a more complete account of the past a reader would need histories from many focuses and, so to say, hold them as overlays in the mind.

The Fascination of History

Copernicus (1473-1543) signalled a revolution in scientific thought when, from his observations, he concluded the Earth was not the centre of the Universe. History's enduring fascination owes much to the necessary centrality of people in historical study. While science and technology enable Man to take an outward journey of exploration to the solar system and beyond, History draws Man to the daunting but exhilarating challenge of understanding human beings and their lives together in society.

The History
Graduate

18 After a Degree

AMONG THE REASONS students undertake a History degree course are their success and enjoyment in History study. A degree will give you more choice in the type of career and a higher place in the hierarchy of work. In a recent survey by York University, only about 8 per cent of History graduates went on to careers, such as teaching or museum work, in which the content of their degree course was more or less directly related. In another study of graduate career direction by Dr Peter Beck and Dr David Stevenson (*Careers Guide for History Graduates*, published by the Historical Association, 1994) they identified the careers History graduates entered (see page 88).

For some other careers, particularly Law, History is a helpful historical background and for all occupations, because History is founded on a study of people, it provides a background to the our Western cultural tradition and a surer appreciation of the present.

Although the great majority of History graduates do not use the content of their degree course in their careers, during study they develop and refine skills - skills which are transferable to later employment work. These skills include:

- The capacity to absorb and manage a good deal of information.
- The capacity to order and analyse information.
- The capacity to reason with clarity and cogency.
- The use and refinement of judgement from evidence.
- The preparation of argument.
- The ability to express an argument persuasively and with clarity.

It is these developed capacities which prepares graduates for successful careers in the areas of finance, management, administration, the media and so on.

Whereas in your parents' generation, at a time of full employment, they could take off to Ladakh or Bogata for a year or

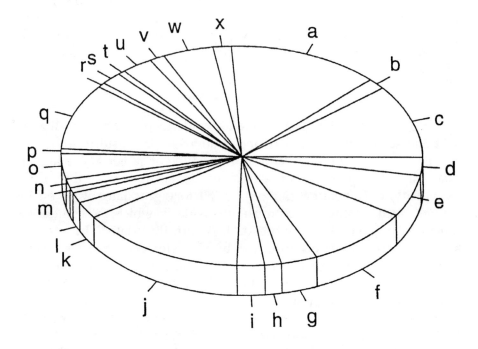

a)	Administration and management	13.4%	
b)	Personnel	1.6%	
c)	Buying, marketing and selling (inc. advertising and public relations)	10.7%	
d)	Management services (including computing and data processing)	2.7%	
e)	Secretarial and clerical	6.3%	
f)	Accountancy	9.4%	
g)	Banking	3.2%	
h)	Insurance	1.5%	
i)	Other financial work (including investment and the Stock Exchange)	2.5%	
j)	Teaching and lecturing	18.8%	
k)	Librarianship	2.5%	
l)	Non-scientific research and information services	1.5%	
m)	Museums and art galleries	0.8%	
n)	Publishing	1.3%	
o)	Journalism	3.9%	
p)	Archive work	0.7%	
q)	Law	9.6%	
r)	Police	0.7%	
s)	Armed Forces	1.9%	
t)	Medical and nursing services	0.7%	
u)	Social, welfare and religious work	2.8%	
v)	Creative and entertaining (including broadcasting, film and theatre)	1.4%	
w)	Manual and non-professional occupations	4.5%	
x)	Other occupations	1.6%	

Figure 18. History graduate career direction, 1988-92 (from Careers Guide *for* History Graduates *by Peter Beck and David Stevenson. Reproduced by courtesy of The Historical Association).*

so secure in the knowledge that they could gain a remunerative and rewarding job within weeks of their return, changes in the global economy have ended these indulgent luxuries and most students seek to start a career when they graduate. Students who begin work on graduation do not necessarily lose out because there are often opportunities to take time out during a career.

Job Applications

If you take the decision to begin a career straight away the time to choose and make application is in January and February of your final year. You do not need to wait, and it is best not to wait, until after you have graduated. Don't expect to be accepted by the first employer to whom you apply for a graduate post. Job applications are time consuming and can be tedious and it takes time away from undergraduate activities and study just when you are preparing to consolidate your course (see Chapter 11), but the more applications you complete the easier it becomes. A useful tip is to make a photocopy of your applictions before you send them. There are two benefits. One is that you can remind yourself what you wrote if you are called for an interview. Second, there may be information or phrases that you can use with later applications. If you do not put aside time in the early spring of your final year, the time employers expect to hear from graduates to be, you can expect greater difficulty and a period of unemployment.

Whatever your chosen career your employer will choose you from the tens or hundreds of applicants for three main reasons: your personality (the undergraduate years offer a great opportunity for you to grow to be a more full and rounded member of society), the transferable skills you developed and refined during your course, mentioned earlier in this chapter, and the work experience you can cite on your CV (see page 4).

It is my hope that you have found this short guide a help to both your success and to your enjoyment as an undergraduate History student. Good luck with your career!

Further Reading

History Study

There are few books dedicated solely to undergraduate History study but seemingly endless general study guides for all levels. A book that can be speedily skimmed and pillaged for ideas is Derek Rowntree, *Learn How to Study*, first published in 1970 by Macdonald but in subsequent editions. Three longer guides, written not only for History students but for the Humanities in general are: Andrew Northedge, *The Good Study Guide*, The Open University, 1990; *Study! A Guide to Effective Study, Revision and Examination Techniques* by Robert Barrass, Chapman and Hall, 1984; and *Successful Study for Degrees* by Rob Barnes, Routledge, 1992. A really useful guide to clear thought and debate is Robert Thouless, *Straight and Crooked Thinking*, first published in 1930 by Hodder and Stoughton but in subsequent editions. Patrick Meredith, *Learning, Remembering and Knowing*, Hodder and Stoughton, 1961, is a concise book which has a different approach and more depth than usual study skills books. Tony Buzan, *Make the Most of Your Mind*, Colt Books, 1977, is nattily presented. It is a popular survey of research on study. For English and expression O.M. Thomson, *A Matter of Style*, Hutchinson, 1973, is excellent: the book is very short and tellingly clear. Plain English by Diané Collinson, Gillian Kirkup, Robin Kyd and Lynne Slocombe, The Open University Press, 1992, will be helpful for students with particular concerns about grammar. M.J. Lewis and Roger Lloyd-Jones, *Using Computers in History. A Practical Guide*, Routledge, 1996, is well illustrated and gives helpful advice on the use of computers with data. *The Good History Students' Handbook*, Sempringham, 1993, has a collection of 17 short but clear definitions of key concepts, terms and ideologies used in History texts which students are likely to read.

Thinking about History

A Companion to the Study of History by Michael Stanford, Blackwell, 1994, is a really helpful point of departure. Written in clear jargon-free prose with a wealth of illuminating examples, the author guides the reader through discussion and provides a wealth of insights. The same author's *The Nature of Historical Knowledge,* Blackwell, 1986, covers similar ground but in a different form. In *History: What and Why? Ancient, Modern and Postmodern Perspectives,* Routledge, 1996, Beverley Southgate plots the direction of the discipline of History in a closely reasoned narrative and argues for a pluralistic future. Authur Marwick, *The Nature of History,* Macmillan, 1970 and later editions, fluently delivers a history of the discipline of History, the relationship with other disciplines and aspects of historical study. *Philosophy of History* by William H. Dray, Prentice-Hall Foundations of Philosophy series, 1964, is a short introduction to the speculative and critical philosophy of History.

Students who explore issues from the theory of History are likely to look at two edited collections of writings: *Theories of History* edited by Patrick Gardiner, The Free Press USA, 1959, and *The Varieties of History. From Voltaire to the Present* edited by Fritz Stern, Macmillan, 1956. Alban G. Widgery, *Interpretations of History. Confucius to Toynbee,* Greenwood Press USA, 1961, is a survey over a wider canvas. *The Philosophy of History* edited by Patrick Gardiner, Oxford - Readings in Philosophy series, 1974, is a collection of essays from the critical philosophy of History.

Individual statements which students are likely to find stimulating include *The Hero in History* by Sidney Hook, Beacon Press USA, 1955, in which the author engages in the debate on determinism and explores the role of particular individuals. Parts of *The Idea of History,* Oxford University Press, 1946, by R.G. Collingwood, encapsulate Collingwood's ideas while Marc Bloch's *The Historian's Craft,* Manchester University Press, 1954, has many insights. H.R. Trevor Roper's valedictory lecture, *History and Imagination,* Clarendon Press, 1980, is an elegant invitation to view the past as it was.

Index

Major themes can be located from the contents page